## Get used to different

**Have you found a spotless lamb for sacrifice?**
-Pharisee to the Shepherd, Pilot Episode

**That's not for you.**
-Jesus to Mary Magdalene, Episode 1

**I was one way and now I'm completely different.**
-Mary Magdalene to Nicodemus, Episode 2

**I hope my next students ask the same questions you do.**
-Jesus to the children, Episode 3

**You have much bigger things ahead of you.**
-Jesus to Simon, Episode 4

**If not now, when?**
-Jesus' mother, Mary, to Jesus, Episode 5

**Please don't turn away from me.**
-Leper to Jesus, Episode 6

**Everything I thought I knew, what if it's wrong?**
-Matthew to his mother, Episode 7

**It would be good if you believed me.**
-Jesus to the Samaritan woman, Episode 8

## The Chosen Study Library

For: skeptics... observers... seekers... learners... followers.

### THE CHOSEN STUDY
10 Studies from 8 Episodes in Each Guide

Season 1   Season 2   Season 3   Season 4   Season 5   Season 6   Season 7

WATER   HOPE   FOOD   SIGHT

### THE BIBLE IN THE CHOSEN
20 Studies from 20 Scenes in Each Guide

Season 1   Season 2   Season 3   Season 4   Season 5   Season 6   Season 7

**Find the (eventual) 140 YouTube Chosen Scene Playlist at:**
tinyurl.com/chosen-playlist-1 (others: -2, -3, -4, -5, -6, -7)

# The Chosen Study
## WATER FOR THE THIRSTY

# The Chosen Study
## WATER FOR THE THIRSTY

A welcoming and
Interactive experience for everyone:
observers... skeptics... learners... seekers... followers.

### The Jesus Study Team
Bill & Teresa Syrios, Dietrich Gruen,
Tori Foss, Bill Ditewig, and Don & Cathy Baker

*Watch > Discover > Relate
the Most Audacious
Story ever told.*

*If anyone thirsts, let him come to me and drink.*
-Jesus (John 7:37)

**Crossover Press**

©2023 Water for the Thirsty: The Chosen Study, Season One
New Edition (Ten Studies Inspired by The Chosen)
Bill Syrios & TJS Team

Scripture quotations are from the ESV® Bible (The Holy Bible, English Standard Version®), ©2001 by Crossway, a publishing ministry of Good News Publishers. Used by permission. All rights reserved.

The Jesus Study guides are not
affiliated with *The Chosen* TV show or *Angel Studios*.

ISBN: 978-0-9716683-8-6

"**The Chosen** is a television drama based on the life of Jesus Christ, created, directed and co-written by American filmmaker, Dallas Jenkins. It is the first multi-season series about the life of Christ, and season one was the highest crowd-funded TV series or film project of all time.

The series' creators stated that they had hoped to distinguish the new series from previous portrayals of Jesus by crafting a multi-season, episode-based story. The series portrays Jesus 'through the eyes of those who met him.'" —*The Chosen*, Wikipedia

**The Chosen Study** focuses on *filling out* the series with Scripture passages to take everyone deeper. The guide can profitably be used by individuals with the hope that they... we... facilitate outreach and learning with others in one-on-one and group contexts. After all: *People must know!*

# Contents

Welcome to The Chosen Study, Season One . . . . . . . . . . . . . 8
Study and Discussion Format. . . . . . . . . . . . . . . . . . . . . . . . . .9
A Word as We Begin. . . . . . . . . . . . . . . . . . . . . . . . . . . . . . . 15

### The Studies / Discussions

Study #1: The Shepherd, Pilot Episode 0 . . . . . . . . . . . . . . . .21
    Micah 5:2-5; Isaiah 9:2-7, 35:3-6; Luke 2:1-21

Study #2: I Have Called You by Name, Episode 1 . . . . . . . . . . 37
    Luke 7:36-50

Study #3: Shabbat, Episode 2. . . . . . . . . . . . . . . . . . . . . . . . 49
    Genesis 1:1-2:3; Exodus 2:8-11

Study #4: Jesus Loves the Little Children, Episode 3 . . . . . . . . 63
    Psalm 63; Matthew: 19;13-15, 18:1-6

Study #5: The Rock on Which It Is Built, Episode 4 . . . . . . . . . 75
    Luke 4:38-5:11

Study #6: The Wedding Gift, Episode 5 . . . . . . . . . . . . . . . . . 87
    Luke 2:40-52; John 2:1-12

Study #7: Indescribable Compassion, Episode 6 . . . . . . . . . . .101
    Isaiah 40:3-5; Mark 1:40-2:12

Study #8: Invitations, Episode 7. . . . . . . . . . . . . . . . . . . . . 113
    Numbers 21:4-9; John 3:14-15; 1-21

Study #9: I Am He, Episode 8. . . . . . . . . . . . . . . . . . . . . . .127
    John 4:1-26

Study #10: Integrate Your Chosen Experience, Episode 8B. . .139
    John 4:27-39; Review; Looking Ahead

Your Faith Journey. . . . . . . . . . . . . . . . . . . . . . . . . . . . . . 150
Background Notes . . . . . . . . . . . . . . . . . . . . . . . . . . . . . . 157
Leader's Notes. . . . . . . . . . . . . . . . . . . . . . . . . . . . . . . . .169
Study and Leadership Resources. . . . . . . . . . . . . . . . . . . . . 179

## Welcome to The Chosen Study, Season One

The English word "gospel" comes from the Greek term, *evangelion*, which means "good news." The four gospel (good news) writers wanted their readers to not only know how remarkable Jesus was, but to know how good his message becomes in the lives of those who embrace it.

To understand their message better, we watch, study, and discuss Chosen episodes with complementary biblical passages. So, wherever you may be spiritually—**skeptic... observer... seeker... learner... or follower**—we're glad you've joined in to learn from those who knew Jesus best.

## Flexible Time Options: Food + Film + Scripture + Discussion

**Longer:** WATCH > DISCOVER > RELATE with food, as set out in this guide, takes *2½ to 3 hours*. **This format is most impactful and cited below.** *

**Medium:** If limited to *1½ to 2 hours*, you will need to skip questions or eliminate a "Discover" section to condense and keep up the pace.

**Shorter:** If the group has less time, say *an hour*, you could: 1) watch the episode and 2), study the passages before coming. Then as you meet, you would discuss what you watched and studied in preparation. (This option is less than ideal if members' preparation is inconsistent.)

| *EXAMPLE: Midweek or Sunday | *EXAMPLE: Saturday Morning |
|---|---|
| **5:45 ARRIVE:** 15 min. to gather | **8:45 ARRIVE:** 15 min. to gather |
| **6:00 POTLUCK:** 30 min. relax/eat | **9:00 LITE BREAKFAST:** 30 min. |
| **6:30-8:30** *THE CHOSEN STUDY* | **9:30-11:30** *THE CHOSEN STUDY* |

### Invite Others to Join

Email or text the **3:37 min. trailer** to those interested in coming to your group (also see pages 169-172): tinyurl.com/trailer-season-one

**NOTE FOR EVERYONE:** We use **"tinyurl.com"** to create shortened URLs for you to type into your browser window to access most of the videos.

## GUIDE OVERVIEW: 3-Step Process → Drive it Home

**The Chosen Study guide** provides a means of bringing people together to study and discuss Chosen episodes with Scripture. This framework gives direction to dynamic group studies and discussions:

**PRIOR To STUDY** — **How to Lead the Study**
Tips to help current (and future) leaders prepare. Please fully read pages 17-18.

**1. WATCH** View Episode Together > Discuss — **FROM The CHOSEN**
Questions that take us deeper into the episode.

**2. DISCOVER** Read Passage > Mark It Up > Discuss — **FROM The BIBLE**
Intro, "Look Fors," Questions to grasp meaning.

**3. RELATE** Apply Insights to God, Life, and Yourself > Discuss
Make applications and summarize in a T-Shirt Design.

**T-Shirt Design** Create a memorable one-liner
Crystallize your thoughts in a slogan or drawing.

### GUIDE COMMENTARY & ARTISTIC LICENSE

**Notes on the Study** Commentary and Historical Context
The biblical passages' context and meaning put into perspective.

**REALISTIC But REAL?** That's plausible but did it happen?
The Chosen's artistic license put into perspective.

### PERSONAL FOLLOW-UP AFTER YOUR GROUP

**Drive it Home** and **Video Insights** and **Worship—Pray—Share**

A. C. T. S. Prayer: Adoration/Confession/Thanksgiving/Supplication
S. H. A. R. E. Mentality: Stop/Hear/Analyze/Risk/Execute

## 1) WATCH  View Episode 1 Together (52 min.) > Discuss

Example, Season Two, Episode 1:
   *I Have Called Your by Name*
   Luke 7:36-50

*On next page* →

## 2) DISCOVER  Read Text > Mark It Up > Discuss

General Example, The Word Became Flesh: John 1:1-14

**Ask the "W" Questions**

**WHO** is involved | **WHEN** did it happen | **WHERE** is it happening
**WHAT** is taking place | **HOW** is it happening... and then ask...
**WHY** questions to uncover the author's original meaning.

*The **"Look For"** at the end of each **INTRO** provides initial direction.

**Mark Up the passage(s) by using
a FOUR-COLORED BIC PEN to draw:**

*On next page* →

- Circles around people or places
- Boxes around whatever you'd like
- Lines under key words and phrase
- Clouds wherever you'd feel like it.
- Identify change of scene, watch for contrast, repetition, key words
- Write notes in the margins

## 3) RELATE  Apply to God & Life | After Study:  Drive it Home

**Express Your Thoughts:** *Write, discuss, and live out* applications from the passages in your life— your relationship with God, with others, your values, priorities, goals.

*On page 12* →

Study and Discussion Format | 11

## How to WATCH The Chosen

Go to thechosen.tv and access each season under the "Watch" tab. You can also search for *The Chosen* in your phone's app store or stream it to your smart TV from The Chosen app, or from providers like Prime, Netflix or The CW.

The Chosen

Always **turn on** the *TV's closed captions* to better follow the narrative. **Darken** *the room* to better enhance the action. A big TV also helps!

**Note:** We identify the length of each episode (or segment of a episode) in the WATCH sections to help you pace the study.

Remember, it's better to leave things unsaid than to bog down.

## How to DISCOVER a passage's meaning

**Example from LUKE 7:** ³⁶ One of the Pharisees asked him to eat with him, *To check Jesus out* and he went into the Pharisee's house and reclined at table. ³⁷ And behold, a woman of the city, who was a sinner, when she learned that he *Uninvited & Compelled* was reclining at table in the Pharisee's house, brought an alabaster flask of ointment, ³⁸ and standing behind him at his feet, weeping, she began *Inappropriate in public*   *Note the action words* to wet his feet with her tears and wiped them with the hair of her head and kissed his feet and anointed them with the ointment. ³⁹ Now when the Pharisee who had invited him saw this, he said to himself, "If this man were a prophet, he would have known who and what sort of woman this is who is touching him, for she is a sinner." ⁴⁰ And Jesus answering said to *Inappropriate to Simon* him, "Simon, I have something to say to you." And he answered, "Say it, *Very deliberate personal address* Teacher."...

## How to use the guide's questions: GENERAL then SPECIFIC

Unlike most Bible studies, these studies consider the fact that your group has just spent time studying (*Discover* section). So, instead of using the guide's questions first, **start with "general questions,"** like:

   *... Set the scene, who's involved, and what are they doing?*

   *... What did you see (observe, notice, or appreciate) in this section?*

*... What strikes you (surprises you, or is something new to you) here?*

   **Then, ask general follow-up questions like:** *... Any other thoughts?*

Such questions often lead to an extended back-and-forth dialogue (see page 188). That's your discussion goal. If this happens, **you do not need to use many or any of the guide's more specific questions.** So, if or when the dialogue wanes or wanders from the main points, then you can use some of the guide's **more "specific questions,"** such as:

   *–How did John the Baptist prepare the way for Jesus?*

   *–What did it mean when Peter called Jesus "the Christ"?*

## RELATE and T-Shirt Design for the passage's application

A few questions remain to help apply the text to your life and a T-Shirt Design for summarizing your most important takeaways (see page 23-24). Use these for a group wrap-up.

## Drive it Home and Video Insights and Worship—Pray—Share

Schedule a quiet time during the week after the study—say on "your Sabbath"—to **review and respond** with *worship, prayer* and *sharing*.

The **Drive it Home** section continues with **Video Insights,** which provide a variety of resources, from music videos to word studies to Bible teaching. This will expose you and your group to other growth opportunities. Next comes **ACTS**—*Adoration, Confession, Thanksgiving, Supplication* and **SHARE** on pages 34-35.

Study and Discussion Format | 13

# WATER FOR THE THIRSTY

Whoever drinks of the water that I give him
will never be thirsty again.

-Jesus to the woman at the Well, John 4:14

## A Word as We Begin

***The Chosen*** *is meant to take you into the eyes and ears of the people who followed Jesus. We believe that if you can see Jesus through the eyes of those who met him, you can be changed and impacted in the same way they were. If we can connect you with their burdens and struggles and questions, then ideally, we can connect you to the solution, to the answer to those questions.*
–Dallas Jenkins

One-on-One Get-Togethers   or   Small Group Meetings   or   Small/Large (8+) Group Gatherings

**The Chosen Study** supports these aspirations by pairing The Chosen with Old and New Testament passages to take us deeper—together.
–The Jesus Study Team

## PRIOR to STUDY

### Leading Season One—preparation checklist

**Leader's Note:** *Buy guides and four-colored BIC pens in advance.* Participants can purchase guides themselves but it's often easier if one person buys the guides (from Amazon is easiest) along with four-color BIC pens (find 6 or 12 BIC pen packs on Amazon). We keep the guides affordable to encourage their widespread use. To see all our guides and to order—including **volume discounts**, see: jesusstudy.org/order-guides.

Buy some extra guides for new people and those who forget to bring theirs—it will happen. **Label these as *EXTRA* on the back cover** to use for others in subsequent weeks. Feel free to charge the participants a fee for reimbursement to cover these purchases.

If someone forgets their guide and there are no extras, go to the website **to get the PDF by typing in URL:** jesusstudy.org/season-one

-*Watch the episode, study the passage(s), and take notes* ahead of time. Look at the *Notes* after the questions (and other commentaries, as you see fit), as well as the *Real But Realistic?* sections.

-*The Notes* are for reference, not for discussion, unless time allows.

-*Always tell your group at which question to end,* so they know how far to go during the study and discussion time.

-*The Relate question* (page 27) is for personal contemplation and then, with *the T-Shirt design* (pages 28-29), meant to be drawn and shared with the group at the end of your study. Have fun with it!

-*Keep up the pace!* Time can pass more quickly than you expect, so watch the clock, leave things unsaid, and keep moving to finish on time. (Ask your group's permission to interrupt to keep up the pace!)

-*Prepare by using Prior To Study* on page 18, and before each study.

**Page 18 is the template. All other studies follow a similar pattern.**

## Leading Study #1—facilitating checklist

-Begin by exchanging names and personal info. Put together a sign-up sheet. (See pages 177-178 and sign-up sheet on website under *Resources*.)

-Have members put their names on the back cover for identification.

-Identify your time constraints and group size. (See pp. 8, 15 and 172.)

-Go through the Eight Ground Rules on page 173. Talk about signing **The Ground Rules #8 Challenge** of consistent attendance. We're not here to lay on guilt, but constancy serves us all. Have fun with stressing this!

-Talk through the study format by going through pages 10 to 12, so that everyone has a feel for the M-I-U and the guide's overview.

-Read or summarize the Intro and the "Look For" on page 22 and have a prepared volunteer read aloud the passages (pages 22-24).

-Give members time for personal study using four-color BIC pens. Monitor to end study time when appropriate. **Keep up the pace!**

-Discuss the first four passages by asking general discussion questions, then specific ones in small/large group as time allows (see page 12).

-Watch the Chosen pilot episode and discuss (page 25).

-Have a prepped volunteer read the Intro and passage (pages 25-27) and give members some time for personal study using BIC pens. Monitor group(s) to end study time when appropriate. **Keep up the pace!**

-Discuss the passage by asking general, then specific questions (p. 12).

-Spend time reflecting on, writing, and sharing the Relate questions, and the T-Shirt Design (pages 27-29). Then share these in the group.

-Point out the Drive it Home, Video Insights, ACTS and SHARE sections (pages 32-35) for your group. Encourage a midweek (or Sabbath) review.

**Leaders:** What are the key things for you to focus on?

- 
- 
- 
- 
- 
- 
- 
- 
- 

**The Chosen, 40 Days with Jesus:** *The Chosen* produces a devotional for each season which can be used five days a week over the course of the study. We highly recommend it. (See page 182 for more info.)

**The Bible Project:** Some of our studies include videos from *The Bible Project*. You can find their large video collection on books of the Bible, biblical themes, word studies, animated outlines and commentary of biblical books. See: bibleproject.com

**The Bible Artist:** Kevin Keating has a notable website with extensive resources on film and Scripture study with a focus on *The Chosen*. See: thebibleartist.com

# The Shepherd (Pilot Episode)

**BACKGROUND:** From the beginning, *The Chosen* has been unusual. Born out of the seeds of a Hollywood box office flop, the creator, Dallas Jenkins, wondered if he had what it took to ever make an appealing movie.

Dallas's church asked him to create a short film for Christmas (aka, *The Shepherd,* now the Pilot episode), and from this film he and the Angel Studios team went on to initiate the largest crowdfunded media production in history—to the tune of over 10 million dollars given by 75,346 enthusiastic fans: Season One of *The Chosen*.

The plan continued: Have each season crowdfund the next one until they complete all seven seasons. The series is free and funded by people interested in "paying it forward." And now it's time to watch it, study it, discuss it, and live it forward.

**NOTE FOR EVERYONE:** To hear Dallas talk about the story behind *The Chosen*, see: tinyurl.com/chosen-story. It's good!

To help him with historical context, Dallas has engaged an Evangelical, Messianic Jew, and Catholic scholar. You can access their interviews for each episode at tinyurl.com/roundtable-discussion.

## DISCOVER  Read Aloud > Mark It Up > Discuss

**INTRO:** Old Testament prophets anticipated the coming Messiah. In Study #1's pilot episode, we are introduced to two such prophets quoted in four different texts. But there's a problem: ***Were the Jewish leaders looking for the right Messiah?*** (For historical background on these prophecies, see the Notes on pages 30-31.)

**Look For: Underline the words describing the One coming.**

### The Ruler to Be Born in Bethlehem

> **MICAH 5** ² But you, O Bethlehem Ephrathah,
>> who are too little to be among the clans of Judah,
>
> from you shall come forth for me
>> one who is to be ruler in Israel,
>
> whose coming forth is from of old,
>> from ancient days.
>
> ³ Therefore he shall give them up until the time
>> when she who is in labor has given birth;
>
> then the rest of his brothers shall return to the people
>> of Israel.... ⁵ And he shall be their peace.

### For to Us a Child Is Born

> **ISAIAH 9** ² The people walking in darkness
>> have seen a great light;
>
> on those living in the land of deep darkness
>> a light has dawned.
>
> ³ You have enlarged the nation
>> and increased their joy;
>
> as warriors rejoice

when dividing the plunder.
⁴ For as in the day of Midian's defeat,
    you have shattered
the yoke that burdens them,
    the bar across their shoulders,
    the rod of their oppressor.
⁵ Every warrior's boot used in battle
    and every garment rolled in blood
will be destined for burning,
    will be fuel for the fire.
⁶ For to us a child is born,
    to us a son is given,
    and the government will be on his shoulders.
And he will be called
    Wonderful Counselor, Mighty God,
    Everlasting Father, Prince of Peace.
⁷ Of the greatness of his government and peace
    there will be no end.
He will reign on David's throne
    and over his kingdom,
establishing and upholding it
    with justice and righteousness
from that time on and forever.
    The zeal of the Lord Almighty
will accomplish this.

## The Ransomed Shall Return

**ISAIAH 35** ³ Strengthen the weak hands,
and make firm the feeble knees.
⁴ Say to those who have an anxious heart,
"Be strong; fear not!
Behold, your God
will come with vengeance,
with the recompense of God.
He will come and save you."
⁵ Then the eyes of the blind shall be opened,
and the ears of the deaf unstopped;
⁶ then shall the lame man leap like a deer,
and the tongue of the mute sing for joy.
For waters break forth in the wilderness,
and streams in the desert

## The Sign of Immanuel

**ISAIAH 7** ¹⁴ Therefore the Lord himself will give you a sign.
Behold, the virgin shall conceive and bear a son,
and shall call his name Immanuel.

**1.** *How do these prophets describe the Messiah and his coming?*

**WATCH** View Pilot under *The Shepherd: A story of the first Christmas* (19 min., :40 to 19:30: tinyurl.com/c-shepherd) or on YouTube (search: The Chosen: Shepherd) > **Discuss**

**INTRO:** *The Shepherd* (pilot episode) asks and, to some degree, answers what kind of Messiah the Jewish nation and the world should expect.

**2.** From the film, how would you describe the shepherd's encounter:

... with the religious leaders?

... with Joseph and Mary?

... with the angelic hosts?

... with the baby Jesus?

**DISCOVER** Read Aloud > Mark It Up > Discuss

**INTRO:** The affairs of state get interrupted by the affairs of heaven in a Bethlehem manger. An unprepared world receives a unique baby boy.

*Use the "W" questions (page 10) and look for the action words.*

### The Birth of Jesus Christ

**LUKE 2** In those days a decree went out from Caesar Augustus that all the world should be registered. ² This was the first registration when Quirinius was governor of Syria. ³ And all went to be registered, each to his own town.

⁴ And Joseph also went up from Galilee, from the town of Nazareth to Judea, to the city of David, which is called Bethlehem, because he was of the house and lineage of David, ⁵ to be registered with Mary, his betrothed, who was with child. ⁶ While they were there, the time came for her to give birth. ⁷ And she gave birth to her firstborn son and wrapped him in swaddling cloths and laid him in a manger, because there was no place for them in the inn.

**The Shepherds and the Angels**
⁸ And in the same region there were shepherds out in the field, keeping watch over their flock by night. ⁹ And an angel of the Lord appeared to them, and the glory of the Lord shone around them, and they were filled with great fear. ¹⁰ And the angel said to them, "Fear not, for behold, I bring you good news of great joy that will be for all the people. ¹¹ For unto you is born this day in the city of David a Savior, who is Christ the Lord. ¹² And this will be a sign for you: you will find a baby wrapped in swaddling cloths and lying in a manger." ¹³ And suddenly there was with the angel a multitude of the heavenly host praising God and saying,

> ¹⁴ "Glory to God in the highest, and on earth
> peace among those with whom he is pleased!"

¹⁵ When the angels went away from them into heaven, the shepherds said to one another, "Let us go over to Bethlehem and see this thing that has happened, which the Lord has made known to us." ¹⁶ And they went with haste and found Mary and Joseph, and the baby lying in a manger. ¹⁷ And when they saw it, they made known the saying

that had been told them concerning this child. ¹⁸ And all who heard it wondered at what the shepherds told them. ¹⁹ But Mary treasured up all these things, pondering them in her heart. ²⁰And the shepherds returned, glorifying and praising God for all they had heard and seen, as it had been told them.

²¹ And at the end of eight days, when he was circumcised, he was called Jesus, the name given by the angel before he was conceived in the womb.

**3.** There are both *ordinary* and *cosmic* elements to the story of Jesus' birth. *What stands out to you about his birth?*

**4.** Bethlehem is about six miles south of Jerusalem and 80-90 miles from Nazareth (see maps on pages 166-167). *What do you imagine that Joseph's and Mary's journey and accommodations were like?*

**5.** *How does the story of Jesus' birth help us understand the nature and role of the Messiah?*

**RELATE**  How It Applies to God, Life, and You > Discuss

**6.** *If you had never heard of this story* before, *what would appeal to you, surprise you, or even make you uncomfortable?*

## 28 | The Chosen Study, Season One

**T-Shirt Design** After watching > discovering > relating, what slogan would you write or draw on your T-Shirt?

**NOTE FOR EVERYONE:** End by completing the RELATE section and designing your T-shirt. Then share them with your group. On the first page, under *Come and See* (as well as below), are some T-shirt sayings. Feel free to get more creative...or not with your design and share it!

### Example concepts/quotations summarizing the film:

Hey guys, thanks for taking the time to write it down!

In the beginning. . . John plagiarized the Book of Genesis.

My most important right: being God's child. Granted, it's granted.

OR

You could DRAW a picture that summarizes your thoughts.

**T-Shirt Design** After watching > discovering > relating, what slogan would you write or draw on your T-Shirt? Wrap up by sharing with your group.

**Draft concepts/quotations for summarizing this study:**

Final design:

**NOTE FOR EVERYONE:** Don't be shy. Share what you created for your T-Shirt. Which other slogans or drawings you particularly like from others in your group?

## Notes on Study #1 — Commentary and Historical Context

### Micah 5:2-5—The Ruler to Be Born in Bethlehem Ephrathah

- There are two Bethlehem's. A southern one (Ephrathah) and a northern one. Micah proclaimed his messages against spiritual decay in Samaria and Jerusalem during the reigns of Jotham (742-735 BC), Ahaz (735-715 BC) and Hezekiah (715-686 BC). The Assyrians conquered Israel's northern ten tribes in 721 BC and deported many of her citizens. In the face of failure, Micah raises the hope of God's salvation, embodied in a coming ruler to be born in a small village.

### Isaiah 9:2-7—For to Us a Child Is Born

- As the northern kingdom was about to be attacked and taken into captivity, the southern kingdom, under King Ahaz, entered a time of increasing distress and darkness as a vassal state of Assyria (eventually conquered by Babylon in 586 BC). With national collapse on the horizon, Isaiah proclaimed the coming of the Messiah to lead his people to victory and to bring an era of joy and peace.

- Who would be the one to overthrow these oppressors and banish war? Shockingly, God will raise up a child—a newborn, no less—to deliver his people and establish justice. This child is not part of an earthly government, but he carries with him a heavenly one.

### Isaiah 35:3-6—The Ransomed Shall Return

- Jesus begins his ministry in his hometown of Nazareth by claiming the power that Isaiah prophesied over 700 years earlier would attend the Messiah's coming. (Compare Isaiah 35:3-6 and Isaiah 61:1-2 with Luke 4:18-19.)

- Jesus makes his Messianic legitimacy clear to John the Baptist who, in prison, wondered if he really was the Messiah. When John's disciples put this question to Jesus, he answered them, *Go and tell John what you hear and see: the blind receive their sight, and the lame walk, and lepers are cleansed, and the deaf hear, and the dead are raised up, and the poor have good news preached to them. And blessed is the one who is not offended by me* (Matthew 11:4-6).

**Isaiah 7:14— The Sign of Immanuel**
- The promised child is virgin-born, named *Immanuel*: God with us!

**Luke 2:1-21—The Birth of Jesus Christ**
- Jesus' story is unlike Greek mythology. It is rooted in history during the noteworthy reign of Caesar Augustus (31 BC – 14 AD), the great-nephew of Julius Caesar. After eventually besting his rivals, Augustus brought about a peaceful and thriving rule, the *Pax Romana*.

- "When Quirinus was governor of Syria" (2:2) is another historical anchor. Joseph and Mary travel nearly 90 miles from Nazareth to their ancestral home, Bethlehem, to register for a census. Luke tells the story of ordinary people caught up in a grand, cosmic event.

*That's plausible but did it happen?*

**Was there a once-lame shepherd who first saw Jesus?** We have no such reference. One would not be surprised, however, if the Messiah's arrival could have had such an impact on those who encountered him (Again, see Isaiah 35:3-6. Compare to Matthew 11:4-6 and Luke 4:18-19).

**Did that shepherd share water with Mary before the birth of Jesus?**
We don't know. Joseph and Mary were likely expecting to stay with relatives or in an inn after their long trip. Once there, they found no place for the birth except a stable. A small act of kindness, however, fits the theme of God providing water for the thirsty, and foreshadows a theme developed in Episode 8, with a role reversal of sorts.

## 32 | The Chosen Study, Season One

**Drive it Home** Review and Respond: Worship, Pray, Share

Review study. Enjoy a worship video to enhance your sense of gratitude of the mercy-filled events in Bethlehem 2,000 years ago.

*Christmas Day* –Chris Tomlin and We The Kingdom
**Type in URL** tinyurl.com/christmas-day-song (4:20 min.)

*Linus' Christmas Speech* –From Charlie Brown
**Type in URL** tinyurl.com/linus-christmas-speech (1:50 min.)
(Note when Linus drops his blanket!)

*O Little Town of Bethlehem* –Chris Tomlin
**Type in URL:** tinyurl.com/little-town (3:44 min.)

7. The word "audacious" means surprisingly bold, risky, impudent, even lacking respect. *In what way was Jesus' birth audacious?*

8. How were the circumstances of Jesus unimpressive to most?

9. How does Jesus' birth story make him more appealing to you?

**Study #1, The Shepherd | 33**

**Video Insights** *The Birth of Jesus: Luke 1-2* -The Bible Project
**Type in URL:** tinyurl.com/the-birth-of-jesus  (5:05 min.)
**Thoughts:** _____




*Oh Little Town of Bethlehem* -Skip Heitzig
**Type in URL:** tinyurl.com/micah5-bethlehem  (42:08 min.)
**Thoughts:** _____




*The Misunderstood "Immanuel" in Matthew* -The Bible as Art
**Type in URL:** tinyurl.com/immanuel-misunderstood  (8:23 min.)
**Thoughts:** _____

## A. C. T. S. Prayer:
Adoration / Confession / Thanksgiving / Supplication

Examine where you are with the Lord and the priorities of his kingdom. Take it to him in prayer:

ADORATION: How can you praise God from whom all blessings flow?




CONFESSION: What do you need to confess and change?




THANKSGIVING: Which circumstances will you thankfully embrace?




SUPPLICATION: For whom and for what will you pray?




. . . ANYTHING ELSE:

## S. H. A. R. E. Mentality:
### Stop / Hear / Analyze / Risk / Execute

Apply what you are learning to your opportunities, then take bold action to serve. What is a situation that you want or need to:

**STOP:** Take a moment to get focused. What is the issue to address?

**HEAR:** Listen not to the urgent, but the important. What is that?

**ANALYZE:** Determine the obstacles and options. How will you proceed?

**RISK:** Resist the familiar and easy. What's your growing edge here?

**EXECUTE:** Move from the mental to the real. What will you do next?

Getting ready for the next study

**NOTE FOR LEADERS:** Begin by having new people introduce themselves.

Then, right before your group studies the passage in Luke 7 (page 39), reiterate the study process on pages 10-12.

**NOTE FOR EVERYONE:** This guide assumes no prior preparation, but there is a place for "post-study reflection" called:

### Drive it Home

You have seen this for Study #1 on pages 32-35 and will see it for the next study on pages 44-47. Schedule a **God-encounter time** during the week to review and respond to your last study experience. We have included worship videos and questions to go deeper.

You also likely noted the section called:

### Insight Videos

These videos are meant to give you a feel for the wide variety of available video resources. Such content provides even more biblical insight and historical context to the passages being studied.

To access them, it is necessary to be precise when typing in their URL into your computer, tablet, or phone's browser window. Our website has direct links at jesusstudy.org, under *Study Options—Season One*.

Finally, pages 46-47 are for post-study prayer and "next steps" action:

### A-C-T-S
### S-H-A-R-E

# I Have Called You by Name (Episode 1)

**Study #2**

**INTRO:** We begin in 2 BC with **Mary Magdalene** as a little girl being comforted by her father. The episode then transitions to 26 AD, 28 years later. Mary is possessed by seven demons (Luke 8:2), and in such distress that her name (in *The Chosen*) had been changed to Lilith, a name that means "night monster" (see page 44).

Along the way, we meet several characters that develop the storylines further: **Quintus**, the Roman Praetor of Galilee; **Nicodemus**, a Jewish Pharisee, both concerned about Jews who are fishing on *Shabbat* (the Sabbath) but for different reasons; Nicodemus' wife, **Zohara**; **Matthew**, a despised Jewish tax collector; his Roman centurion escort, **Gaius**; the fishermen brothers, **Andrew** and **Simon**; plus, Simon's wife, **Eden**.

## 38 | The Chosen Study, Season One

**WATCH** View Episode 1 (52 min. from 0:00 to 52:20) > **Discuss**

1. From the film's depiction, what stood out to you about each person, their situation, and dilemma:

   ... Simon and Andrew?

   ... Matthew?

   ... Nicodemus?

2. How would you characterize Mary's situation when we first met her as a young girl? And now, 30 years later?

3. Note the Scripture that Mary's father used to comfort her as a girl, and that Jesus speaks to her (leaving off "O Jacob" and O Israel"):

   "Thus says the Lord, he who created you, O Jacob, he who formed you, O Israel: Fear not, for I have redeemed you; I have called you by name, you are mine" (Isaiah 43:1}.

   What struck you about Mary's encounter with Jesus in the tavern and his quoting of Isaiah 43:1 to her?

## Study #2, I Have Called You By Name | 39

**DISCOVER** Read Aloud > Mark It Up > Discuss

**INTRO:** Mary Magdalene is from Magdala, a fishing town on the western shore of the Sea of Galilee. She is referenced twelve times in the New Testament. In Luke 8:2-3, the author lists her as one of the women who traveled with Jesus and helped support him.

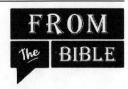

That same passage says that seven demons were driven out of her. Mary ends up being a witness to the Crucifixion, the empty tomb and the first to see the risen Christ—"the Peter of the women." Possibly, she is the woman described in this passage. Whether it is really her or not, this story describes well the kind of person Mary Magdalene becomes.

**Look especially for the contrasts between characters in this passage.**

### Jesus' Message: A Debt, Forgiveness and Love

**LUKE 7:** [36] One of the Pharisees asked Jesus to eat with him, and he went into the Pharisee's house and took his place at the table. [37] And behold, a woman of the city, who was a sinner, when she learned that he was reclining at table in the Pharisee's house, brought an alabaster flask of ointment, [38] and standing behind him at his feet, weeping, she began to wet his feet with her tears and wiped them with the hair of her head and kissed his feet and anointed them with the ointment.

[39] Now when the Pharisee who had invited him saw this, he said to himself, "If this man was a prophet, he would have known who and what sort of woman this is who is touching him, for she is a sinner."

[40] And Jesus answering said to him, "Simon, I have something to say to you. "And he answered, "Say it, Teacher." [41] "A certain moneylender had two debtors. One owed five hundred denarii, and the other fifty. [42] When they could not pay, he cancelled the debt of both. Now which of them will love him more?"

⁴³ Simon answered, "The one, I suppose, for whom he cancelled the larger debt."

And he said to him, "You have judged rightly."

⁴⁴ Then turning toward the woman he said to Simon, "Do you see this woman? I entered your house; you gave me no water for my feet, but she has wet my feet with her tears and wiped them with her hair. ⁴⁵ You gave me no kiss, but from the time I came in she has not ceased to kiss my feet. ⁴⁶ You did not anoint my head with oil, but she has anointed my feet with ointment. ⁴⁷ Therefore I tell you, her sins, which are many, are forgiven—for she loved much. But he who is forgiven little, loves little."

⁴⁸ And he said to her, "Your sins are forgiven."

⁴⁹ Then those who were at table with him began to say among themselves, "Who is this, who even forgives sins?"

⁵⁰ And he said to the woman, "Your faith has saved you; go in peace."

**4.** *What stood out to you about this dinner party?*

**5.** *How would you contrast Simon (the Pharisee) with the woman?*

**6.** A 500 denarii debt equals two years of salary and a 50 denarii debt, two months' salary. *What does this parable illustrate about the two debtors?*

**7.** Jesus contrasts Simon's and the woman's actions toward him. *How do their responses show their understanding of their debt, the forgiveness offered, and the response made?* Use the chart if helpful.

|  | **Simon** | **Woman** |
|---|---|---|
| Amount of Debt (Recognized)? | | |
| Forgiveness Offered/Received? | | |
| Response Made? | | |

**8.** Why is Simon unable to recognize that he is a debtor?

**9.** What was Jesus' message to Simon?

... his message to the woman?

### RELATE   How It Applies to God, Life, and You > Discuss

**10.** How would, or does, a recognition of being forgiven affect your view of others and of God?

**NOTE FOR EVERYONE:** End by completing the RELATE questions and the T-Shirt design individually and then sharing them in your group.

**T-Shirt Design** After watching > discovering > relating, what slogan would you write or draw on your T-Shirt? Wrap up by sharing with your group.

Draft concepts/quotations for summarizing this study:

Final design:

## Notes on Study #2 — Commentary and Historical Context

### Luke 7:36-50—Jesus' Message: A Debt, Forgiveness and Love

- The issue of being religious but unloving (Simon) versus being non-religious—"a sinner"—but loving (the woman), challenges us. With whom do we identify most? Do we come to God on our own terms, in self-righteous pride—or on his terms, in humility?

- What Simon didn't do was considered a customary greeting when an honored guest arrived at one's home.

- The issue that love is a result of experiencing forgiveness, not the other way around, is seen in the woman's motivation. When it comes to God, we don't start by loving, we start by being loved.

- The gospel message is well portrayed in the story and in the parable: (1) We all have an *unpayable debt* (as sinners); (2) *debt is canceled* (through forgiveness); resulting in (3), a *transformed response* (love).

### That's plausible but did it happen?

**Was Simon married?** Yes, as he had a mother-in-law (Mark 1:29-31), but we don't know his wife's name or any specifics about her.

### Did Matthew collect taxes from fishermen like Simon and Andrew?
We do not know from Scripture, but it's likely. Matthew was a tax collector operating around the Sea of Galilee (Mark 2:13-14). His concern about these two particular fishermen being able to "square their account" would have been an ongoing concern for any Jewish business under the heavy hand of Roman taxation.

### Did Nicodemus travel to Galilee to teach students?
Maybe, but he met Jesus in Jerusalem, not Capernaum (John 2:29–3:1) and we have no reference to his students.

### Did Nicodemus try to heal Mary Magdalene?
Mary was delivered from seven demons (Luke 8:1-2), but there is no record of Nicodemus ever meeting her, nor where it took place.

**Is Zohara, the wife of Nicodemus, in the gospel record?**
She is not mentioned, but her character in *The Chosen* helps to demonstrate the divergence of opinions about Jesus, which are beginning to surface between Nicodemus and others in his circle.

**Is there significance in Mary's name, *Lilith*, when possessed?**
Yes, Lilith was a demonic figure in Jewish folklore whose name was thought to derive from a class of Mesopotamian demons and meant "night monster" with a cult following that lasted to the 7$^{th}$ Century. But we do not know what her demon-possessed name was or even if she had one. Regardless, Mary is completely cleansed of their influence.

**Drive it Home** Review and Respond: Worship, Pray, Share

Rewatch the encounter between Jesus and Mary Magdalene, personalize through song as a reminder of God's redeeming love in your life.

*The Chosen's Mary Magdalene, Rescue* –Lauren Daigle
**Type in URL:** tinyurl.com/needing-rescue (3:48 min.)

*I Speak Jesus* –Charity Gayle
**Type in URL:** tinyurl.com/I-speak-Jesus (7:46 min.)

11. *On the following continuum, put an "X" on the line in the place that best describes your relationship with God (Jesus) right now.*

---

Observer...    Skeptic...    Learner...    Seeker...    Follower...

12. *Do you want to move further to the right on the spectrum as shown above? If so, what might that mean for you?*

13. *Who could help, and what could you do to encourage such growth?*

**Study #2, I Have Called You By Name | 45**

**Video Insights** *Good News from Luke 7:36-50* –Bill Syrios
**Type in URL:** jesusstudy.org/good-news-from-luke-7 (24:33 min)
**Note:** At this link there is a PDF of this study to be used with a friend.
**Thoughts:**

*Forgiveness Leads to Love* –John Piper
**Type in URL:** tinyurl.com/forgiveness-leads-to-love (12:05 min.)
**Thoughts:**

*What is the Gospel?* –Melissa Dougherty (This is an excellent video!)
**Type in URL:** tinyurl.com/the-gospel-defined (20:24 min.)
**Thoughts:**

## A. C. T. S. Prayer:
Adoration / Confession / Thanksgiving / Supplication

Examine where you are with the Lord and the priorities of his kingdom. Take it to him in prayer:

ADORATION: How can you praise God from whom all blessings flow?



CONFESSION: What do you need to confess and change?



THANKSGIVING: Which circumstances will you thankfully embrace?



SUPPLICATION: For whom and for what will you pray?



... ANYTHING ELSE:

**S. H. A. R. E.** Mentality:
*Stop / Hear / Analyze / Risk / Execute*

Apply what you are learning to your opportunities, then take bold action to serve. What is a situation that you want or need to:

**STOP:** Take a moment to get focused. What is an issue to address?


**HEAR:** Listen for what's truly important. What are those things?


**ANALYZE:** Determine the pitfalls and obstacles. How will you proceed?


**RISK:** Resist the familiar and easy. What's your growing edge here?


**EXECUTE:** Move from the mental to the real. What will you do next?

The Shabbat Reading

**NOTE FOR LEADERS:** One way to **start the study** is to ask group members what is something that they valued from the previous week's ***Drive it Home*** segment after the study.

**NOTE FOR EVERYONE:** This reading is recited before partaking of the *Shabbat* (Sabbath) meal, exalting God's creation and Israel's blessing.

*Now the heavens and the earth were completed, and all their hosts, and God completed on the seventh day all His work that He did. And God abstained on the seventh day from all the work He did. And God blessed the seventh day, and He hallowed it, for thereon He abstained from all the work that God created to do. Blessed are you, Lord our God, Ruler of the universe, who created the fruit of the vine. You have lovingly and willingly given us your Shabbat as an inheritance in memory of creation. Because this is the first day of our holy assemblies in memory of the Exodus from Egypt. Blessed are you, Lord our God, King of the universe, who brings forth the bread from the earth. Amen*

### Eshet Chayil
*Ode to Women of Valor*
*that also exalts the rhythm of work and rest.*

Proverbs 31:10-31 is, likewise, recited or sung before the Shabbat meal as praise to women, and a blessing to children. *Valor can be defined as a great force of courage.* The Ode begins as follows:

> *A woman of valor, who can find?*
> *Her worth is far beyond that of jewels....*

# Shabbat (Episode 2)

**Study #3**

FROM The BIBLE

**INTRO:** The *Shabbat* (aka the Sabbath) was given to Israel 4,000 years ago as a practice that celebrates God "resting" on the seventh day from the work of Creation. This example acts as a weekly reminder for his people to slow down, reassess, and focus on what is most important: our family, our friends, our calling, and God himself.

Let's slow down ourselves to look at God's six days of work in creation and the seventh day pattern of rest that he set for those he made in his image.

*Look for: Use one color to underline what is the same on each day; with another color highlight what is different each day. (Or circle, box or cloud it—your call!)*

> **DISCOVER**  Read Aloud > Mark It Up > Discuss

**The Creation of the World (... a condensed version)**

**GENESIS 1** In the beginning, God created the heavens and the earth. ² The earth was without form and void, and darkness was over the face of the deep. And the Spirit of God was hovering over the face of the waters.

³ And God said, "Let there be light," and there was light. ⁴ And God saw that the light was good. And God separated the light from the darkness. ⁵ God called the light Day, and the darkness he called Night. And there was evening and there was morning, **the first day**.

⁶ And God said, "Let there be an expanse in the midst of the waters, and let it separate the waters from the waters." . . . ⁸ And God called the expanse Heaven. And there was evening and there was morning, **the second day**. . . . ¹⁰ And God saw that it was good.

¹¹ And God said, "Let the earth sprout vegetation, plants yielding seed, and fruit trees bearing fruit in which is their seed, each according to its kind, on the earth." . . . ¹² And God saw that it was good. ¹³ And there was evening and there was morning, **the third day**.

¹⁴ And God said, "Let there be lights in the expanse of the heavens to separate the day from the night. And let them be for signs and for seasons, and for days and years. . . . ¹⁸ And God saw that it was good. ¹⁹ And there was evening and there was morning, **the fourth day**.

²⁰ And God said, "Let the waters swarm with swarms of living creatures, and let birds fly above the earth across the expanse of the heavens." . . . ²¹ And God saw that it was good. ²² And God blessed them, saying, "Be fruitful and multiply and fill the waters in the sea . . . . "
²³ And there was evening and there was morning, **the fifth day**.
²⁴ And God said, "Let the earth bring forth living creatures according to their kinds." . . . ²⁵ And God saw that it was good.

²⁶ Then God said, "Let us make man in our image, after our likeness. And let them have dominion over the fish of the sea and over the birds of the heavens and over the livestock and over all the earth and over every creeping thing that creeps on the earth."

²⁷ So God created man in his own image, in the image of God
he created him; male and female he created them.
²⁸ And God blessed them. And God said to them, "Be fruitful and multiply and fill the earth and subdue it," . . . ³¹ And God saw everything that he had made, and behold, it was very good. And there was evening and there was morning, **the sixth day**.

### The Seventh Day, God Rested
**GENESIS 2** Thus the heavens and the earth were finished, and all the host of them. ² And on **the seventh day** God finished his work that he had done, and he rested on the seventh day from all his work that he had done. **³ So God blessed the seventh day and made it holy, because on it God rested from all his work that he had done in creation.**

## Remember the Sabbath

**EXODUS 20** [8] "Remember the Sabbath day, to keep it holy. [9] Six days you shall labor, and do all your work, [10] but **the seventh day** is a Sabbath to the Lord your God. On it you shall not do any work, you, or your son, or your daughter, your male servant, or your female servant, or your livestock, or the sojourner who is within your gates. [11] **For in six days the Lord made heaven and earth, the sea, and all that is in them, and rested on the seventh day. Therefore, the Lord blessed the Sabbath day and made it holy.**

1. "In the beginning": The first thing God created was time. He then set aside six days (or periods of time) to craft creation.
   *What stands out to you about his process of creating our world?*

   *... about the mention of his pleasure ("it was good") in the process?*

   *... about the creation of humanity on Day Six?*

2. *What do you learn about the origin and meaning of the Sabbath on Day Seven?*

**3.** The thought of God "resting" is rather unusual. *What do you think this reference implies?*




**WATCH** View Episode 2 *(38 min., from 1:25 to 39:17)* **> Discuss**

**INTRO: Nicodemus** *(teacher of teachers)* is a member of the Sanhedrin, the Jewish high court that included 70 members. The **Av Beit Din** presided as its second highest-ranking member  and *The Chosen* includes him also visiting Capernaum. Nicodemus' students, **Shmuel** and **Yussif,** make another appearance, and we are introduced to Jesus' first two students, **"Little" James** and **Thaddeus.**

**4.** *What stood out to you about each of their situations or dilemmas as expressed in the four Shabbat meals:*

*... for Matthew and his dog?*



*... for Simon, Eden (Simon's wife), and Andrew?*



*... for Nicodemus, Zohara, and company?*



*... for Mary, Jesus, and company?*

5. What did you think of how Mary describes her changed life to Nicodemus, and later, her introduction of Jesus to her guests as "the man who helped me?"

**WATCH** View BibleProject.com video: Sabbath (5 min.) > Discuss (tinyurl.com/sabbath-bible-project)

6. From this video, how would you describe the expanded meaning and purpose of the Sabbath?

7. How would Sabbath rest differ from sleep or being on vacation?

**RELATE** How It Applies to God, Life, and You > Discuss

8. How might you make better use of the Sabbath as a weekly reset, including the reminder of God's presence and his work around us?

Study #3, Shabbat | 55

**T-Shirt Design** After watching > discovering > relating, what slogan would you write or draw on your T-Shirt?

Draft concepts:

Final design:

**NOTE FOR EVERYONE:** This upcoming week provides an opportunity to establish "your own Sabbath." And yes, we have the ideal plan for part of it! Carve out some time to review and respond to the previous study's content. (What day and time are best for you?)

After looking back over the last study, engage with the worship and teaching videos provided. Go deeper with the A-C-T-S and S-H-A-R-E exercises. Encourage others in your group from your experience.

## Notes on Study #3 — Commentary and Historical Context

**Genesis 1:1-31—The Creation of the World**
- The word for "day" in Hebrew is *yom*. This word's meaning is not precise and depends on its context. So, whether this period of Creation was six 24-hour days or six billion years, each increment is poetically celebrated as *good*...and finally *very good*.

**Genesis 2:1-3—The Seventh Day, God Rested**
- God honors his six days of work with a seventh day of rest, which he blessed and made "holy," (meaning *set apart*). How appropriate he rests right after creating humanity—uniquely made in his image and commended to help him manage his creative work!

**Exodus 20:8-11—Remember the Sabbath**
- It's hard to fathom what it means that the Creator of the Universe somehow paused to rest. As the meaning of the Sabbath becomes increasingly clear in Exodus 20:8-11 and beyond, his actions are more for us, his creatures, as a model for living well. **Question:** *If we can't work 1/7 of our potential amount of work time, how will we make it?* **Answer:** *By depending on God, that he will come through for us.*

That's plausible but did it happen?

**Did the Jews save a seat for Elijah during the Passover?** Yes, observant Jews do this during Passover (not every Sabbath) to honor the expectation that Elijah would come again to herald the Messiah (Malachi 4:5). Jesus indicates, however, that John the Baptist fulfilled this expectation of Elijah's ministry (Matthew 11:14).

**Were the disciples as young as Matthew looks?**
Quite likely Jesus' disciples were young—perhaps most were under age 18, some as young as 15. The reasons for this are deduced from Jewish tradition, historical context, and a few clues from Scripture. In Jesus' day, a Jewish man received a wife after age 18. Simon was the only one known to have been married. (In Matthew 8:14-15, it was his mother-in-law, named Dasha. in this film, whom Jesus healed.)

So, we may presume the others were young—either teens, too young to be married, or slightly older bachelors, but still young, without the family responsibilities Simon had.

The tradition of education, which formally ended at age 15 at that time, also indicates a youthful band of brothers. Higher education (for those wealthy or gifted enough) consisted of studying under a local rabbi who accepted some very young men as students; otherwise, they entered the workforce by their mid-teens, usually apprenticed under their fathers in the family business.

**Was there an issue of Jews fishing on the Sabbath?**
Unsure, but it's reasonable to assume so. Jews were under Roman occupation, so when it came to avoiding paying taxes, you can be assured that they searched for any possible way out, which for some, meant violating the Sabbath. Episode 4 will expand on this issue.

**Did Simon betray the other fishermen?**
There is no record that he had a *tax problem,* so there would have been no reason for him to consider betraying his fellow Jews.

**NOTE FOR EVERYONE:** It is not an unfair development for *The Chosen* writers to give Simon a sense of desperation—having massive, unpaid taxes. And desperate times can call for desperate measures—wagering on fights or selling out fellow fishermen to the Romans. But, while this backstory makes for an intriguing and even plausible storyline, we have no biblical evidence that Simon had tax debts in the first place.

**The potential problem stems from the powerful, visual nature of film (and the music score behind it) that can easily sweep us up and have us assign meaning from it to the written word. We would say, do both: study what the Scripture actually says, and enjoy the captivating ride *The Chosen* takes us on—but learn the difference!**

If you'd like more input on this, check out Dallas' videos, *Can you trust The Chosen?* and the *Interview of Jonathan Roumie*, the actor who portrays Jesus. See page 168 for more info and those video links.

## Drive it Home — Review and Respond: Worship, Pray, Share

Rewatch **Sabbath** – The Bible Project
**Type in URL:** tinyurl.com/sabbath-bible-project (5:27 min.)

Watch, listen, sing and praise with a worship video that declares: *Praise to the Lord, the Almighty, the King of Creation.*

**Praise to the Lord (Joyful, Joyful)** – Shane and Shane
**Type in URL** tinyurl.com/praise-to (4:37 min.)

**House Of The Lord** – Phil Wickham
**Type in URL** tinyurl.com/house-of-the-lord (4:14 min.)

9. Set aside time to evaluate your schedule and your pace of life and ask: *How well am I living according to my priorities?*

10. *What changes will you consider making:*

   ... *in your relationship with God?*

   ... *in the lives of key family members (spouse, children, etc.)?*

   ... *in how you are living your life or spending your time?*

**Video Insights** *Genesis 1 -The Bible Project*
**Type in URL:** tinyurl.com/genesis-one (7:42 min.)
**Thoughts:**

*The Jewish Observation of Shabbat*
**Type in URL:** tinyurl.com/the-shabbat *-Rabbi Jason Sobel*
**Thoughts:** (9:03 min.)

We'd highly recommend watching the video below and to incorporate the **Drive it Home** sections into your own upcoming "Sabbaths."

*Sabbath, The Command Christians are Ok Violating*
**Type in URL:** tinyurl.com/value-the-sabbath *-Robert Morris*
**Thoughts:** (30:20 min.)

## A. C. T. S. Prayer:
Adoration / Confession / Thanksgiving / Supplication

Examine where you are with the Lord and the priorities of his kingdom. Take it to him in prayer:

ADORATION: How can you praise God from whom all blessings flow?




CONFESSION: What do you need to confess and change?




THANKSGIVING: Which circumstances will you thankfully embrace?




SUPPLICATION: For whom and for what will you pray?




... ANYTHING ELSE:

**S. H. A. R. E.** Mentality:

*Stop / Hear / Analyze / Risk / Execute*

Apply what you are learning to your opportunities, then take bold action to serve. What is a situation that you want or need to:

STOP: Take a moment to get focused. What is the issue to address?


HEAR: Listen not to the urgent, but the important. What is that?


ANALYZE: Determine the obstacles and options. How will you proceed?


RISK: Resist the familiar and easy. What's your growing edge here?


EXECUTE: Move from the mental to the real. What will you do next?

### It's not too late

**QUESTION and ANSWER FOR EVERYONE:**

*Inviting new people—is it too late?*

No, it isn't. One of the beautiful things about *The Chosen Study* is that new members can come in at any time and binge watch to catch up! Additionally, we've seen people go through each Season's episodes multiple times.

#### Who to invite?

Anyone who fits on this list: friends, loved ones, family members, colleagues, teammates, acquaintances, those who cross your path—if they're curious, if they're willing to check it out—then invite them to come.

# Jesus Loves The Little Children (Episode 3)

## Study #4

**INTRO:** If life is difficult, then spirituality (inviting God into the mix) can be that much more challenging and compelling. The studies in this guide end at a well where a woman is offered living water for her thirsty soul. Like her, our lives can feel like we're living in a "desert," if not perpetually, at least for a season, as we encounter experiences that leave us emotionally and spiritually dry.

Jesus looked to the Father in such circumstances to reveal truth, gain wisdom, and find strength. He encourages us to do the same—to trust and embrace him through life's twists and turns, in its confusion and pain. Never be afraid to take his hand and let him lead.

**DISCOVER** Read Aloud > Mark It Up > Discuss

**Look for the personal pronouns and to whom or to what they are connected.**

**A psalm of David. When he was in the Desert of Judah.**
**PSALM 63**

> ¹ You, God, are my God,
>> earnestly I seek you;
> I thirst for you,
>> my whole being longs for you,
> in a dry and parched land
>> where there is no water.
>
> ² I have seen you in the sanctuary
>> and beheld your power and your glory.
>
> ³ Because your love is better than life,
>> my lips will glorify you.
>
> ⁴ I will praise you as long as I live,
>> and in your name I will lift up my hands.
>
> ⁵ I will be fully satisfied as with the richest of foods;
>> with singing lips my mouth will praise you.
>
> ⁶ On my bed I remember you;
>> I think of you through the watches of the night.
>
> ⁷ Because you are my help,
>> I sing in the shadow of your wings.
>
> ⁸ I cling to you;
>> your right hand upholds me.

**1.** *How does the Psalmist describe his current condition?*

**2.** *How does he remind himself of God's provision for him?*

**3.** *How does the reminder of God's love strengthen his (and your) heart?*

**WATCH** View Episode 3 *(28 min., from 0:00 to 28:23)* > *Discuss*

**INTRO:** The irrepressible **Abigail**, and her friend, **Joshua** "the Brave," lead a group of children who spend the entire episode with Jesus. Losing their initial shyness, the group is put to work by Jesus, and they find themselves becoming his most inquisitive students.

**4.** *What stood out to you about the questions the children ask Jesus?*

**5.** *How does he teach them in a playful and purposeful way?*

## DISCOVER  Read Aloud > Mark It Up > Discuss

**INTRO:** Who doesn't love children? Well, the disciples seem to have serious issues with them. Granted, children can be inconvenient, but not so to Jesus. Not only is he drawn to "the least of these," he also recognizes the power that childlike meekness and openness has as an object lesson for faith.

*Look for the comparisons and note them.*

**Matthew 19:** $^{13}$ Then children were brought to him that he might lay his hands on them and pray. The disciples rebuked the people, $^{14}$ but Jesus said, "Let the little children come to me and do not hinder them, for to such belongs the kingdom of heaven." $^{15}$ And he laid his hands on them.

**Who Is the Greatest?**
**Matthew 18:** The disciples asked Jesus, "Who is the greatest in the kingdom of heaven?"

$^2$ And calling to him a child, he put him in the midst of them $^3$ and said, "Truly, I say to you, unless you turn and become like children, you will never enter the kingdom of heaven. $^4$ Whoever humbles himself like this child is the greatest in the kingdom of heaven.

$^5$ "Whoever receives one such child in my name receives me, $^6$ but whoever causes one of these little ones who believe in me to sin, it would be better for him to have a great millstone fastened around his neck and to be drowned in the depth of the sea.

**6.** *What is the difference between the disciples' approach and Jesus' approach with these children?*

**7.** What about children makes them good object lessons for faith?

**8.** Jesus calls his disciples to "turn" in verse 3. *What are they to turn from and turn toward?*

**RELATE** How It Applies to God, Life, and You > Discuss

**9.** What is it about those with "childlike faith" that disarms and draws us in?

**10.** Who is a "child" in your life who models faith?

*...How could their childlike faith serve you well in your relationship with God?*

**T-Shirt Design** After watching > discovering > relating, what slogan would you write or draw on your T-Shirt? Wrap up by sharing with your group.

Draft concepts/quotations for summarizing this study:




Final design:

**NOTE FOR EVERYONE:** Consider **pairing up** with someone in your group and meeting one-on-one to work on the *Drive It Home* section together at a place of your choosing. This helps in getting to know each other.

## Notes on Study #4 — Commentary and Historical Context

**Psalm 63—A psalm of David. When he was in the Desert of Judah.**

- The Judean wilderness occupies the area from the eastern slopes of the Judea Mountains down to the Great Rift Valley, and runs along the western shore of the Dead Sea. Very little rain falls there (about one inch per year) so there are very few plants or animals.

- According to traditional rabbinic commentaries, this Psalm was composed by David when he fled into the wilderness to escape from King Saul, who wished to kill him. He is using the barrenness of the wilderness to speak of the barrenness of his own soul and his longing to again feel God's presence.

David lived in continual danger, thus fear may have kept him awake and given him wearisome nights. We imagine that he seldom slept two nights in the same bed, but he could comfort himself with thoughts of his connection with God.

- David lifted up his hands in praise (v. 4). The Jewish people are very uninhibited in their worship and praise. We know David entered Jerusalem later leaping and dancing before the Lord with nearly nothing on (2 Samuel 6:14). Hey, being king has its privileges. It is safe to say that we are typically more reserved in our worship style than was David. but hopefully no less genuine!

**Matthew 19:13-15; 18:1-5—Who's the greatest?**

- When pressed by Abigail in this episode, "What is your reason for being here?" Jesus tells the children what he will tell his hometown synagogue based on the words of Isaiah 61 (vv. 18-19). This scene will be shown in Season Three, Episode 3. For now, these children introduce us to the key ingredient of genuine faith: humility.

The disciples can't seem to learn this lesson: Jesus is the champion of the weak. And in that society, indeed, in all societies, the weakest members are the youngest. To him, children are not distractions; their rank makes them role models of living life as Jesus-followers. So, when a dispute arose about status, what better object lesson?!

**That's plausible but did it happen?**

**Did Jesus pray with such anguish to the Father?**
He often withdraws from crowds to be alone with the Father (Mark 1:35) so this depiction is consistent with his practice of prayer.

**Did Jesus camp out on his own, and later, with the disciples?**
Again, we have no record of Jesus setting up a camp like this, but he did say, "The Son of Man has no place to lay his head" (Luke 9:58). We know he stayed in homes at times, but we do not know much about his housing situation or how often he camped out.

**Did Jesus hang out with children like this?**
We have no record of Jesus befriending specific children, but it would not at all be surprising (Matthew 18:1-6; 19:13-15; 21:14-17).

**Would Jesus have made wooden toys?**
Unsure, but he grew up as a son of a carpenter and likely did.

**What is the "Shema" that the children recited?**
The "Shema" is Deuteronomy 6:4-9 (including 11:13-21 and Numbers 15:37-41). It is a confession that faithful Jews recited twice daily. *Shema* is the word "hear" that begins Deuteronomy 6:4.

**Drive it Home** Review and Respond: Worship, Pray, Share

This episode of *The Chosen* depicts Jesus in intense prayer with his Father. This Psalm (song) describes well such prayer for all of us.

*We Will Wait on You (Psalm 130)* –Shane and Shane
**Type in URL:** tinyurl.com/psalm-130-song (6:28 min.)

*Amazing Grace* –Chris Tomlin
**Type in URL:** tinyurl.com/amazing-grace-song (5:47 min.)

11. In what ways do you struggle with humility?

*Whoever humbles himself like this child is the greatest in the kingdom of heaven.... And whoever would be great among you must be your servant.* -Matthew 18:4; 28:26

**12.** *How does this "formula" help you strive for greatness in your life?*

*Clothe yourselves, all of you, with humility toward one another, for "God opposes the proud but gives grace to the humble."* -1 Peter 5:5

**13.** *How does "this formula" prompt you to strive for a grace-filled life?*

**Video Insights** *The Upright Walk of a Bowed Down Man*
**Type in URL:** tinyurl.com/grace-to-humble (42:30 min.) –Skip Heitzig
**Thoughts:** _____

## A. C. T. S. Prayer:
Adoration / Confession / Thanksgiving / Supplication

Examine where you are with the Lord and the priorities of his kingdom. Take it to him in prayer:

ADORATION: How can you praise God from whom all blessings flow?




CONFESSION: What do you need to confess and change?




THANKSGIVING: Which circumstances will you thankfully embrace?




SUPPLICATION: For whom and for what will you pray?




... ANYTHING ELSE:

# Study #4, Jesus Loves The Little Children | 73

## S. H. A. R. E. Mentality:
### Stop / Hear / Analyze / Risk / Execute

Apply what you are learning to your opportunities, then take bold action to serve. What is a situation that you want or need to:

**STOP:** Take a moment to get focused. What is the issue to address?


**HEAR:** Listen not to the urgent, but the important. What is that?


**ANALYZE:** Determine the obstacles and options. How will you proceed?


**RISK:** Resist the familiar and easy. What's your growing edge here?


**EXECUTE:** Move from the mental to the real. What will you do next?

### Reminders

**NOTE FOR LEADERS:** One way to **start your study** is to ask group members about something they valued from the previous week's *Drive it Home* and *Video Insights* segments after study.

**During the study:** Always tell the group at **which question to end**, so they know how far to go during the study time.

**Keep up the pace.** You often think you have more time than you do, so, closely monitor your time, leave things unsaid, and keep moving to finish on time.

**Evaluate as you go:** *What things are working well, and what can be improved in your study and group discussion process?*

# The Rock on Which It Is Built (Episode 4)

## Study #5

**INTRO:** In this episode, we meet fishing business owner **Zebedee,** and his two sons, **"Big" James** and **John** ("Sons of Thunder" in Mark 3:17), along with several Pharisees and their students.

The **Pharisees** were a lay religious order who began around 160 BC, with good intentions of reviving Israel's adherence to Old Testament law. Unfortunately, by Jesus' day, those intentions had turned legalistic, as they followed their own traditions (see Mark 7:13) more than the Old Testament. Some have compared them to strict fundamentalists, in their legalistic concerns about dos and don'ts regarding Sabbath-keeping and other finer points of the Law.

**WATCH** View Episode 4 *(47 min., from 0:00 to 46:43)* > **Discuss**

Simon lives in Capernaum on the Sea of Galilee (also called the lake of Gennesaret). **See maps (and mark the locations) on pages 166-167.** In this episode, he appears to be *caught up in his own net*. Before we read about the resolution in Luke 5, consider these questions:

**1.** *How does the film depict Simon's crisis:*

   *... with the Romans, depicted by Quintus?*

   *... with his brother, Andrew?*

   *... with his wife, Eden?*

   *... with God?*

**2.** Nicodemus, too, is having a crisis. *What are the changes happening in his worldview and faith?*

**DISCOVER**   Read Aloud > Mark It Up > Discuss

**INTRO:** Jesus had Simon's attention, but now he was looking for a full commitment and vocational change with great purpose. If Jesus could make such a difference in Simon's life, maybe there was hope for his contemporaries—and for us.

*The Chosen* takes liberties with the timeline of this passage. We have no indication from the Gospels, for instance, that Simon had a tax debt (see page 57).

*Identify the action words. Use a different color for each character.*

**Jesus Heals Many and Calls Some**

**LUKE 4:** [38] He left the synagogue and entered Simon's house. Simon's mother-in-law was ill with a high fever, and they appealed to him on her behalf. [39] And he stood over her and rebuked the fever, and it left her, and immediately she rose and began to serve them.

[40] When the sun was setting, all those who had any who were sick with various diseases brought them to him, and he laid his hands on every one of them and healed them. [41] And demons also came out of many, crying, "You are the Son of God!" But he rebuked them and did not allow them to speak, because they knew that he was the Christ….

**LUKE 5:** [1] On one occasion, while the crowd was pressing in on him to hear the word of God, he was standing by the lake of Gennesaret, [2] and he saw two boats by the lake, but the fishermen had gone out of them and were washing their nets. [3] Getting into one of the boats, which was Simon's, he asked him to put out a little from the land. And he sat down and taught the people from the boat.

[4] And when he had finished speaking, he said to Simon, "Put out into the deep and let down your nets for a catch."

[5] And Simon answered, "Master, we toiled all night and took nothing! But at your word I will let down the nets."

[6] And when they had done this, they enclosed a large number of fish, and their nets were breaking. [7] They signaled to their partners in the other boat to come and help them. And they came and filled both the boats, so that they began to sink.

⁸ But when Simon Peter saw it, he fell down at Jesus' knees, saying, "Depart from me, for I am a sinful man, O Lord." ⁹ For he and all who were with him were astonished at the catch of fish that they had taken, ¹⁰ and so also were James and John, sons of Zebedee, who were partners with Simon.

And Jesus said to Simon, "Do not be afraid; from now on you will be catching men." ¹¹ And when they had brought their boats to land, they left everything and followed him.

3. In Luke 4:38-39, Simon had witnessed the healing of his mother-in-law, but apparently does not respond to Jesus at that time. *Why does he now?*

4. *Why do you think Simon reacted so strongly?*

5. Note the title change from "Master" (v. 5) to "Lord" (v. 8). *Why is coming to grips with Jesus being Lord (even of his fishing business) so frightening, even defeating to him?*

**RELATE** How It Applies to God, Life, and You > Discuss

6. *Where is Jesus in relation to "your fishing business"—defined as central issues in your life—job, family, future goals, relationships:*

Study #5, The Rock on Which It Is Built | 79

a) nowhere in sight right now
b) on the horizon
c) approaching the boat
d) one foot in, one foot out
e) fully committed, all in    ... Explain your self-evaluation:

**T-Shirt Design** After watching > discovering > relating, what slogan would you write or draw on your T-Shirt?

Draft concepts:

Final design:

| Notes on Study #5 | Commentary and Historical Context |

### Luke 5:1-11—Receiving a Change of Vocation

- Simon sees his mother-in-law healed (Luke 4:38-44), so he knows of Jesus' power, though maybe he is not completely convinced.

- Jesus is a carpenter, and Simon, a fisherman. Jesus' instructions to recast their nets would make no sense to an experienced fisherman. Apparently, Simon needed Jesus' intervention in an aspect of his life in which he considered himself an expert.

- It could be asked: *What does sin have to do with a large haul of fish?* Simon now understands who he's dealing with and who he is in comparison. His response reminds us of Isaiah's personal encounter with God in the Temple. Upon experiencing God's glory, Isaiah declares: *Woe is me! For I am lost; for I am a man of unclean lips, and I dwell in the midst of a people of unclean lips; for my eyes have seen the King, the Lord of hosts!* (see Isaiah 6:1-9).

- Like Isaiah, Simon (now called Peter in v. 8) is given a calling—one that is a grand vocation: to join Jesus as a "fisher of men." Fear is not appropriate, given that he has now united in purpose with Jesus.

 *That's plausible but did it happen?*

**Did John the Baptist call the Pharisees "snakes"?**
Yes, a "brood of vipers," in fact (Luke 3:7). John was eventually thrown into prison by Herod, not the Romans (Matthew 14:1–12; Mark 6:14–29). We have no record of Nicodemus visiting him in prison.

**Did the Romans hire Matthew to "spy" on Simon?**
Doubtful. We know that Matthew collected taxes in the region of Galilee, where Simon and Andrew lived. We do not know if they knew each other before Jesus called them together, although it is possible.

**Did Andrew try to convince Simon, his brother, about Jesus?**
Yes: *The first thing Andrew did after meeting Jesus was to find his brother and tell him, 'We have found the Messiah!* (John 1:41). However, unlike the plot of *The Chosen*, Simon goes right away to Jesus, and Jesus changes his name to "Peter" (1:42).

**Did Matthew witness the miraculous catch of fish?**
We have no record of Matthew being among those whom Jesus taught from the boat. (Nor do we know if he witnessed the healing of the paralytic.) However, he very likely encountered Jesus prior to his response of following Jesus when called from his tax booth.

**What about *The Chosen*'s timeline regarding the disciples?**
Simon and Andrew, along with other disciples, followed Jesus *before* the miraculous catch of fish recorded in Luke 5. So, although *The Chosen* depicts the catch as Simon's first meeting with Jesus, he had prior encounters. Likewise, *The Chosen* depicts his mother-in-law being healed *after* the catch, but (spoiler alert for Episode 8), this took place *before* the catch (Mark 1:30-31).

**Was Simon motivated by tax debt?** We also have no indication in Scripture that Simon (renamed Simon *Peter* by Luke in 5:8) was driven to do what he did by a tax debt. Still, there is no doubt that he was transformed by the miraculous catch and, along with the other fishermen, commits to following Jesus wholeheartedly with the new vocation of drawing people to Jesus and his message.

| Drive it Home | Review and Respond: Worship, Pray, Share

Watch, listen and sing along to this classic hymn written in 1826.
*Holy, Holy, Holy (We Bow Before You)* -Shane and Shane
**Type in URL:** tinyurl.com/holy-holy-holy (7:41 min.)

Watch a compilation of Peter's life thus far in *The Chosen* put to music.
*Peter: Get Back Up—Chosen Music Video* -TobyMac
**Type in URL:** tinyurl.com/get-back-up (3:26 min.)

7. *How does being in the presence of the Almighty radically alter your view of who he is and who you are?*

8. Go back to question #6 again for a longer period of consideration. *Where is Jesus in relation to "your fishing business"—defined as central issues in your life—job, family, future goals, relationships:*
   a) nowhere in sight right now
   b) on the horizon
   c) approaching the boat
   d) one foot in, one foot out
   e) fully committed, all in   ... *Explain your self-evaluation:*

8. Jesus offers Simon a new vocation—catching people—and invites him to go "all in." *What would it take for you to "join Jesus" in a similar, all-in way? Be specific.*

9. Jesus also gives Simon a word of encouragement: "Do not be afraid" (v.10). *If you personalize Jesus' words, what do they mean to you in making an all-in commitment to him?*

**Video Insights** Why Did Jesus Call Fishermen? –Chad Bird
**Type in URL:** tinyurl.com/why-fishermen (24:21 min.)
**Thoughts:**
_____


In Pursuit of Peter, Episode 2 –Our Daily Bread
**Type in URL:** tinyurl.com/pursuing-peter-2 (20:58 min.)
**Thoughts:**
_____


Six Things You Didn't Know about Peter –Brandon Robbins
**Type in URL:** tinyurl.com/info-on-peter (16:57 min.)
**Thoughts:**
_____

## A. C. T. S. Prayer:
Adoration / Confession / Thanksgiving / Supplication

Examine where you are with the Lord and the priorities of his kingdom. Take it to him in prayer:

ADORATION: How can you praise God from whom all blessings flow?




CONFESSION: What do you need to confess and change?




THANKSGIVING: Which circumstances will you thankfully embrace?




SUPPLICATION: For whom and for what will you pray?




... ANYTHING ELSE:

## S. H. A. R. E. Mentality:
### Stop / Hear / Analyze / Risk / Execute

Apply what you are learning to your opportunities, then take bold action to serve. What is a situation that you want or need to:

**STOP:** Take a moment to get focused. What is the issue to address?

**HEAR:** Listen not to the urgent, but the important. What is that?

**ANALYZE:** Determine the obstacles and options. How will you proceed?

**RISK:** Resist the familiar and easy. What's your growing edge here?

**EXECUTE:** Move from the mental to the real. What will you do next?

*Plan ahead now for your last (11th) study!*

**FOR LEADERS AND EVERYONE:** There are some helpful and fun options for planning an 11th study. Please check out page 138 now to acquaint yourself with these options.

If you and your group decide to do something *different* than a normal (11th) meeting, make sure everyone checks their schedules. You want as many of your members there as possible. Again, check out page 138!

## The Wedding Gift (Episode 5)

**Study #6**

FROM The BIBLE

**INTRO:** It would be fascinating to know more about Jesus as he grew up in Nazareth with a humble, gracious mother, a God-fearing carpenter for a dad, and at least six siblings—four named brothers and at least two unnamed sisters (Matthew 13:55-56).

Of course, given the Bible's description of the Holy Spirit's involvement in Mary's pregnancy, they would be Jesus' half-brothers and sisters—same mother, different fathers! And, it should be noted, that Catholic tradition suggests Jesus' siblings were actually "cousins," or relatives, or possibly children from a first marriage of Joseph.

Regardless of your view on Jesus' family, everything the Bible tells us about his growing up years is found in one short passage: Luke 2:40-52. Observe all you can!

*Use your pen to follow the progression in this passage with a special focus on the words "and" and "when."*

**DISCOVER** Read Aloud > Mark It Up > Discuss

### The Boy Jesus in the Temple

**LUKE 2:** [40] The child grew and became strong, filled with wisdom. And the favor of God was upon him.

[41] Jesus' parents went to Jerusalem every year at the Feast of the Passover. [42] And when he was twelve years old, they went up according to custom.

[43] And when the feast was ended, as they were returning, the boy Jesus stayed behind in Jerusalem. His parents did not know it, [44] but supposing him to be in the group they went a day's journey, but then they began to search for him among their relatives and acquaintances, [45] and when they did not find him, they returned to Jerusalem, searching for him. [46] After three days they found him in the temple, sitting among the teachers, listening to them and asking them questions. [47] And all who heard him were amazed at his understanding and his answers.

[48] And when his parents saw him, they were astonished. And his mother said to him, "Son, why have you treated us so? Behold, your father and I have been searching for you in great distress."

[49] And he said to them, "Why were you looking for me? Did you not know that I must be in my Father's house?" [50] And they did not understand the saying that he spoke to them.

[51] And he went down with them and came to Nazareth and was submissive to them. And his mother treasured up all these things in her heart. [52] And Jesus increased in wisdom and in stature and in favor with God and man.

1. All parents can identify with the panic that comes from losing a child in a crowd. *What do you find surprising about this story?*

2. *What else do you learn about Jesus' parents and him as a boy?*

**WATCH** View Episode 5 *(53 min., from 1:48–54:24)* > *Discuss*

**INTRO: John the Baptist** languishes in prison, giving **Nicodemus** an opportunity to question him. (For more on John, see pages 80, 101, 107, and 160.) This time it is about *miracles*—an interview that began in Episode 4. Maybe John knows something about the source of this person and the power that does things he cannot un-see.

In the aftermath of the fish miracle, Eden finds out from her husband, Simon, about a new call on his life and lends her support. This is followed by a water-into-wine miracle. This miracle saved wine stewards, **Thomas** (a future disciple) and **Ramah** (a fictitious character in *The Chosen*), from dreadful humiliation at a wedding party. (For more on Thomas, see pages 95 and 163.)

**3.** What is Nicodemus's question, and John the Baptist's answer regarding apparent miracles?

**4.** How did Simon describe the miracle he had witnessed?

**5.** Why do you think Eden is so affirming of Simon's new calling to follow Jesus?

---

**DISCOVER** Read Aloud > Mark It Up > Discuss

**INTRO:** *The Chosen's* version of the water-into-wine miracle contains plenty of lighthearted moments: tension between the bride's relatively poor family and the groom's rich parents, Jesus  playing with children, the disciples telling stories about how they first met Jesus, and the astonishment of those who saw the miracle.

The account we find in John's Gospel is much more concise. Of course, John could have "played it up," but his straightforward style lends credence to his integrity as an author of historical events. *The Chosen* is "happy" to embellish his just-the-facts narrative, and we are happy to study the source while engaging our imagination as well!

***Observe interaction and highlight the words spoken by each character.***

### The Wedding at Cana

**JOHN 2:** On the third day there was a wedding at Cana in Galilee, and the mother of Jesus was there. ² Jesus also was invited to the wedding with his disciples. ³ When the wine ran out, the mother of Jesus said to him, "They have no wine."

⁴ And Jesus said to her, "Woman, what does this have to do with me? My hour has not yet come."

⁵ His mother said to the servants, "Do whatever he tells you."

⁶ Now there were six stone water jars there for the Jewish rites of purification, each holding twenty or thirty gallons.

⁷ Jesus said to the servants, "Fill the jars with water." And they filled them up to the brim.

⁸ And he said to them, "Now draw some out and take it to the master of the feast."

So they took it. ⁹ When the master of the feast tasted the water now become wine and did not know where it came from (though the servants who had drawn the water knew), the master of the feast called the bridegroom ¹⁰ and said to him, "Everyone serves the good wine first, and when people have drunk freely, then the poor wine. But you have kept the good wine until now."

¹¹ This, the first of his signs, Jesus did at Cana in Galilee, and manifested his glory. And his disciples believed in him.

¹² After this he went down to Capernaum, with his mother and his brothers and his disciples, and they stayed there for a few days.

**6.** What do you find unusual about this miracle?

**7.** How would you describe Jesus' interaction with his mother?

**8.** What effects did the miracle have on those who were there—like the wedding party, servants, master of the feast, Mary (Jesus' mother), the disciples, Jesus?

**9.** Why do you think Jesus used his divine power to produce such ordinary things such as wine for a wedding, or fish for livelihood?

**RELATE**   How It Applies to God, Life, and You > Discuss

**10.** What has God used to get your attention regarding spiritual things?

**T-Shirt Design** After watching > discovering > relating, What slogan would you write or draw on your T-Shirt? Wrap up by sharing with your group.

Draft concepts/quotations for summarizing this study:

Final design:

| Notes on Study #6 | *Commentary and Historical Context* |

### Luke 2:40-52—The Boy Jesus in the Temple

- Notice the artistic connection made in this episode where the boy Jesus and his mother both state rhetorically: "If not now, when? It's a nice touch and it won't be the last time those words are spoken between them. Yes, we're talking about the end of Season Two!

- Some have wondered how Jesus, who is God, could *grow* (as v. 52 indicates he did)? Jesus, as a human being, needed to grow and mature as all humans do. He had to learn such things as how to walk, speak, read, write and work. He just did so sinlessly!

### John 2:1-12—The Wedding at Cana

- In Jewish culture a wedding was seen as uniquely sanctioned by God and thus worthy of the best of all parties where, hopefully, nothing ruinous happened, such as running out of wine!

- At this wedding in Cana, just a few miles from Jesus' hometown of Nazareth, Jesus becomes, in effect, Mary's "plus one," since her husband, Joseph, had likely passed away by this time.

- Jesus addresses Mary as "Woman," but is not discourteous; the word has no easy English equivalent. A phrase like, "My lady," better captures the respect behind its use here. Jesus' hesitation communicates they have a new relationship now, and that a public miracle is not a decision he will be pressured into performing.

*That's plausible but did it happen?*

**Did Jesus' entire family get invited to the wedding in Cana?** Cana is close to Nazareth and Capernaum (John 2:12; see map on pages 166-167). Given this, Jesus' entire family may have attended. If so, the miracle did not convince them he was someone different than the person they knew growing up. Throughout his lifetime, they remain unconvinced of his identity (Mark 3:21; John 7:2-5).

Possibly, given his previous occupation. He was a carpenter (Mark 6:3) who learned his trade from his dad (Matthew 13:55). The Greek word for *carpenter* can also be translated *craftsman* or *artisan*.

All the items that he made added value to others—from the *ordinary* to the *extraordinary*. Jesus may have made toy boats for children and lock-and-key inserts for doors (as depicted in the film version of reality). And he did the extraordinary by turning water into wine and, in the not-too-distant future, producing a couple of boatloads of fish!

**Would running out of wine have been that embarrassing?**
Yes. The show sets up a rich family vs. poor family wedding which serves to add a degree of drama, but such an event would have been humiliating, and a bad way to start a marriage! The guests often traveled for miles to attend, and such parties could last for days.

**Did Thomas (and Ramah) serve wine at the wedding?**
We have no record of Thomas serving at Cana, nor being called to follow Jesus there. The film's portrayal of Thomas as a "measurer" and "doubter" is consistent with one who later becomes known as "doubting Thomas" (John 11:16; 14:5-6; 20:24-29).

*The Chosen* created the characters of Ramah (the wine steward) and Kafni (her father and vineyard owner), who add a colorful dimension to the story's account and one with whom many can identify.

## Drive it Home — Review and Respond: Worship, Pray, Share

Celebration is God's idea. What do you have to celebrate that comes from your relationship with him? Don't let convention stop you. Get up and dance!

*God's Great Dance Floor* –Chris Tomlin
**Type in URL:** tinyurl.com/dance-floor  (7:09 min.)

*Steal My Show* –TobyMac
**Type in URL:** tinyurl.com/steal-my-show (5:11 min.)

**11.** *What are some of your most painful disappointments in life?*

**12.** We all find ourselves wanting miracles in the ordinary course of our lives. *What is something you would like Jesus to do for you?*

**13.** *When God does not provide the miracle or outcome you desire, how have you, at times, processed disappointment in him?*

**14.** *What would it mean to process those disappointments in a God-honoring and personally healthy way?*

Study #6, The Wedding Gift | 97

**Video Insights** Young Messiah Meets Rabbi  -Erma Winbush
**Type in URL:** tinyurl.com/young-messiah-meets-rabbi (3:26 min)
**Thoughts:**


The Chosen Visits Wedding Miracle Site -Dallas Jenkins
**Type in URL:** tinyurl.com/the-wedding-site (4:03 min.)
**Thoughts:**


The Wedding Explain S1/E5  -Brandon Robbins
**Type in URL:** tinyurl.com/the-wedding-explained (24:46 min.)
**Thoughts:**

## A. C. T. S. Prayer:
Adoration / Confession / Thanksgiving / Supplication

Examine where you are with the Lord and the priorities of his kingdom. Take it to him in prayer:

ADORATION: How can you praise God from whom all blessings flow?




CONFESSION: What do you need to confess and change?




THANKSGIVING: Which circumstances will you thankfully embrace?




SUPPLICATION: For whom and for what will you pray?




. . . ANYTHING ELSE:

Study #6, The Wedding Gift | 99

**S. H. A. R. E.** Mentality:
*Stop / Hear / Analyze / Risk / Execute*

Apply what you are learning to your opportunities, then take bold action to serve. What is a situation that you want or need to:

STOP: Take a moment to get focused. What is the issue to address?


HEAR: Listen not to the urgent, but the important. What is that?


ANALYZE: Determine the obstacles and options. How will you proceed?


RISK: Resist the familiar and easy. What's your growing edge here?


EXECUTE: Move from the mental to the real. What will you do next?

### Getting ready for Study #7

**NOTE FOR EVERYONE:** It is helpful to google: *the names Jesus used for himself*. Such a search will turn up 20, not to mention other ones used to address him, plus those in the book of Revelation, totaling nearly 50.

Besides "Rabbi" and "Teacher," the most common title people used to describe Jesus in the New Testament was *Christ* (Greek for *Messiah*). But Jesus himself almost never used that designation, maybe because his general listeners had such misconceptions of who the Messiah would be. Instead, he preferred the title, *Son of Man*.

Some mistakenly assume this self-designation refers to the human side of Jesus; conversely, *Son of God* designates the divine side. Rather, as Jesus' audience would know, this title *(Son of Man)* is given to the heavenly, Messianic being envisioned in Daniel 7:13-14:

> **The Son of Man Is Given Dominion**
>
> **DANIEL 7** [13] "I saw in the night visions,
> and behold, with the clouds of heaven
> there came one like a **son of man**,
> and he came to the Ancient of Days
> and was presented before him.
>
> [14] And to him was given dominion
> and glory and a kingdom,
> that all peoples, nations, and languages
> should serve him;
> his dominion is an everlasting dominion,
> which shall not pass away,
> and his kingdom one
> that shall not be destroyed.

# Indescribable Compassion (Episode 6)

**INTRO**: Many Jewish leaders were shocked by, and did not understand the ministry of, John the Baptist. Isaiah 40:3-5 will be read in this episode and makes John's role clear. He will be the one who prepares the way for the coming of the Messiah.

When the Messiah shows up in first-century Israel, he acts like and does the very things that the Old Testament foretold about what the Messiah would be like and do.

*Look for: Use your pen to identify the things that are going to happen.*

## DISCOVER  Read Aloud > Mark It Up > Discuss

**Prepare the Way**

**ISAIAH 40:** ³ A voice cries:

> "In the wilderness prepare the way of the Lord;
>
> make straight in the desert a highway for our God.
>
> ⁴ Every valley shall be lifted up,
>
> and every mountain and hill be made low;
>
> the uneven ground shall become level,
>
> and the rough places a plain.
>
> ⁵ And the glory of the Lord shall be revealed,
>
> and all flesh shall see it together,
>
> for the mouth of the Lord has spoken."

1. What do Isaiah's analogies tell you about John the Baptist and his mission?

## WATCH  View Episode 6 (50 min., from 0:00 to 49:48) > Discuss

**INTRO: Salome** is introduced. She is Zebedee's wife and ends up in Jesus' inner circle. Likewise, Eden's mother (Simon's mother-in-law), **Dasha**, makes an appearance and is very sick. Before Season One's conclusion, she will meet Jesus in an unusual way!

**Tamar** (the Egyptian woman) is not mentioned in the Gospels. The show, however, follows the actual events and indeed fleshes out the emotions that those caught up in the story would have experienced.

**2.** *As Jesus' ministry goes public, how does this episode describe:*
   *... Matthew and what he has seen?*



   *... the Pharisees' view of John the Baptist and their rigid view of God?*



   *... Nicodemus witnessing the paralytic's healing?*



---

**DISCOVER**  Read Aloud > Study > Discuss

**INTRO:** Leprosy is a debilitating and disfiguring nerve disease. It can now be cured, but in pre-scientific Israel, it was misunderstood and feared. In fact, the rabbis said it was easier to raise the dead than to cure leprosy. This leper, like the paralytic described next, had no hope of a cure, and was rejected by society (Leviticus 13:46).

**Look for instances of cause and effect.**

**Jesus Cleanses a Leper**
**MARK 1:** ⁴⁰ And a leper came to him, imploring him, and kneeling said to him, "If you will, you can make me clean."

⁴¹ Moved with pity, he stretched out his hand and touched him and said to him, "I will; be clean." ⁴² And immediately the leprosy left him, and he was made clean.

⁴³ And Jesus sternly charged him and sent him away at once, ⁴⁴ and said, "See that you say nothing to anyone, but go, show yourself to the priest and offer for your cleansing what Moses commanded, for a

proof to them." ⁴⁵ But he went out and began to talk freely about it, and to spread the news, so that Jesus could no longer openly enter a town, but was out in desolate places, and people were coming to him from every quarter.

**Jesus Heals a Paralytic**
**MARK 2** And when he returned to Capernaum after some days, it was reported that he was at home. ² And many were gathered together, so that there was no more room, not even at the door. And he was preaching the word to them. ³ And they came, bringing to him a paralytic carried by four men. ⁴ And when they could not get near him because of the crowd, they removed the roof above him, and when they had made an opening, they let down the bed on which the paralytic lay. ⁵ And when Jesus saw their faith, he said to the paralytic, "Son, your sins are forgiven."

⁶ Now some of the scribes were sitting there, questioning in their hearts, ⁷ "Why does this man speak like that? He is blaspheming! Who can forgive sins but God alone?"

⁸ And immediately Jesus, perceiving in his spirit that they thus questioned within themselves, said to them, "Why do you question these things in your hearts? ⁹ Which is easier, to say to the paralytic, 'Your sins are forgiven,' or to say, 'Rise, take up your bed and walk'? ¹⁰ But that you may know that the Son of Man has authority on earth to forgive sins"—he said to the paralytic— ¹¹ "I say to you, rise, pick up your bed, and go home." ¹² And he rose and immediately picked up his bed and went out before them all, so that they were all amazed and glorified God, saying, "We never saw anything like this!"

**3.** What strikes you about these back-to-back miracles?

**4.** The leper fails to follow Jesus' instructions. *How does that failure impact Jesus' future ministry?*

**5.** Jesus pronounces the paralytic forgiven and then uses the title, "Son of Man." *How do the Scribes react to this claim and why?*

### RELATE  How It Applies to God, Life, and You > Discuss

**6.** *How has your view of Jesus matured through the years?*

**7.** *In what ways do you still struggle in trusting him to come through for you?*

**T-Shirt Design** After watching > discovering > relating, What slogan would you write or draw on your T-Shirt? Wrap up by sharing with your group.

Draft concepts/quotations for summarizing this study:

Final design:

## Notes on Study #7 — Commentary and Historical Context

### Isaiah 40:3-5—Prepare the Way

- Leaving the cities for the wilderness is an exercise in purging oneself from distractions. As a word picture, the metaphor of building a road in rough terrain is like the preparation one makes to get ready for God's appearance. It is the very role that John the Baptist took on for the people of Israel, to prepare for Jesus' coming.

### Mark 1:40—2:12—Jesus Cleanses and Heals

- Jesus wants the leper's witness to God's power proclaimed through the normal dictates of the Old Testament for such a healing. The second story not only identifies Jesus' power over sickness and disease, but it also reveals that this power is divine. This is shown by the disdain of Scribes (religious lawyers) for Jesus' claim that he can do what only God can do—forgive sins. For this alleged "blasphemy," they "call him out."

### That's plausible but did it happen?

**Did the catch of fish satisfy Simon's and Andrew's taxes?** We have no indication from Mark's Gospel that these fishermen (disciples) had tax debts and thus, shouldn't read this into their motivations. But this high-value haul likely went to Simon's and the others' families to financially sustain them in their absence while traveling with Jesus.

### Did Jesus grow up in Egypt and speak Egyptian?

Joseph and Mary fled to Egypt to avoid the massacre of baby boys under Herod (Matthew 2:13-15). Then they returned to Nazareth after Herod's death (2:19-23). They probably lived in Egypt for several years, though there is no evidence that he spoke Egyptian as an adult.

Hebrew was the language spoken in Jewish scholarly and religious circles and, undoubtedly, Jesus knew Hebrew. However, the common tongue spoken in the villages was a much more wide-spread Semitic one, Aramaic. Jesus also could have spoken *Koiné* Greek and some Latin. Like most of his contemporaries, he would have been bilingual.

### Did the Pharisees sell out John the Baptist to the Romans?
No. John confronted Herod Antipas regarding his illicit relationship with his brother's wife, Herodias. This so angered Herodias, that Herod imprisoned John and, at an opportune moment, Herodias appealed for his execution (Matthew 14:1-12; Mark 6:14-29; Luke 9:7-9).

### Did Joseph die before Jesus began his ministry?
Probably, as there's no mention of him after Jesus begins his adult ministry. Joseph is last named in Luke's narration about the boy Jesus in the Temple (Luke 2:48; see on pages 88 and 94).

### Did Nicodemus ask Mary for a meeting with Jesus?
Not likely, but we do know that his meeting with Jesus happened at night (John 3:2).

### Drive it Home | Review and Respond: Worship, Pray, Share

We all have our own story and, because of the human condition, that story will necessarily include pain, sometimes to the point of absolute hopelessness. But Jesus provides a way out of the darkness: HOPE.

**Hope In Front of Me** -Danny Gokey
**Type in URL:** tinyurl.com/it-is-well-song (4:01 min.)

**Living Hope** -Phil Wickham
**Type in URL** tinyurl.com/Jesus-living-hope (4:14 min.)

**8.** The Gospel passage and film episode stir up a lot of emotion. *How were you touched by it?*

*... What do you sense Jesus is telling you about your life-condition?*

**Video Insights** **The Son of Man** -The Bible Project
**Type in URL:** tinyurl.com/son-of-man (5:50 min.)
**Thoughts:**

---

**Meeting John the Baptist** -The Snipe Life
**Type in URL:** tinyurl.com/meet-john-the-baptist (15:05 min.)
**Thoughts:**

---

**Jesus' Authority to Forgive Sin** -John MacArthur
**Type in URL:** tinyurl.com/Jesus-forgives-sin (53:19 min.)
**Thoughts:**

## A. C. T. S. Prayer:
Adoration / Confession / Thanksgiving / Supplication

Examine where you are with the Lord and the priorities of his kingdom. Take it to him in prayer:

ADORATION: How can you praise God from whom all blessings flow?




CONFESSION: What do you need to confess and change?




THANKSGIVING: Which circumstances will you thankfully embrace?




SUPPLICATION: For whom and for what will you pray?




. . . ANYTHING ELSE:

Study #7, Indescribable Compassion | 111

## S. H. A. R. E. Mentality:
### Stop / Hear / Analyze / Risk / Execute

Apply what you are learning to your opportunities, then take bold action to serve. What is a situation that you want or need to:

**STOP: Take a moment to get focused. What is the issue to address?**

**HEAR: Listen not to the urgent, but the important. What is that?**

**ANALYZE: Determine the obstacles and options. How will you proceed?**

**RISK: Resist the familiar and easy. What's your growing edge here?**

**EXECUTE: Move from the mental to the real. What will you do next?**

**Getting ready for your last gathering.**

**NOTE FOR LEADERS:** It will prove helpful to again consider the study process for your group on pages 10-11, and especially the use of the "W questions." These questions make for a useful starting point for personal study, along with the "Look For" clue given right after the INTRO.

# Invitations (Episode 7)

## Study #8

**INTRO:** Jesus explains his identity and purpose to Nicodemus in a unique way. He compares himself to a bronze serpent God had instructed Moses to fashion. This was the means God used to bring healing to the rebellious Israelites during an unusual incident in their 40-year exodus from Egypt.

When Moses lifted the bronze snake up on a pole, those who had been bitten by poisonous vipers could look up at it and be healed. This foreshadows the great redemption Jesus would bring when he, too, would be lifted up on a cross.

***Identify the comparisons between these two passages.***

| DISCOVER | Read Aloud > Mark It Up > Discuss

### The Bronze Serpent

**NUMBERS 21:** ⁴ From Mount Hor they set out by the way to the Red Sea, to go around the land of Edom. And the people became impatient on the way. ⁵ And the people spoke against God and against Moses, "Why have you brought us up out of Egypt to die in the wilderness? For there is no food and no water, and we loathe this worthless food."

⁶ Then the Lord sent fiery serpents among the people, and they bit the people, so that many people of Israel died. ⁷ And the people came to Moses and said, "We have sinned, for we have spoken against the Lord and against you. Pray to the Lord, that he takes away the serpents from us." So, Moses prayed for the people.

⁸ And the Lord said to Moses, "Make a fiery serpent and set it on a pole, and everyone who is bitten, when he sees it, shall live." ⁹ So Moses made a bronze serpent and set it on a pole. And if a serpent bit anyone, he would look at the bronze serpent and live.

### Lifting Up the Son of Man

**JOHN 3:** ¹⁴ And as Moses lifted up the serpent in the wilderness, so must the Son of Man be lifted up, ¹⁵ that whoever believes in him may have eternal life.

**1.** *Describe the story in Numbers 21 and the analogy in John 3.*

*Study #8, Invitations*

**2.** *How does the snake on the pole relate to healing in both passages?*

---

**WATCH** | View Episode 7 *(35 min., from 0:00-35:11)* > *Discuss*

**INTRO:** In the film, Moses' successor, **Joshua**, protests the serpent imagery, to which Moses says he's only doing as God instructs. The serpent on the pole, once looked at, will save the Israelites from deadly snake bites. So also, Jesus will save his people when he is lifted up on the Cross and they place their faith in him.

**3.** *What is the struggle between:*

   *... Nicodemus and his wife, Zohara?*

   *... Matthew and his mother?*

   *... Simon and Jesus, regarding Matthew?*

---

**DISCOVER** | Read Aloud > Mark It Up > Discuss

**INTRO:** What follows is one of the weightiest passages in Scripture, indeed one of the most significant conversations in human history. Nicodemus was more than a devoted Pharisee; he was one of only 70 elite members of the Sanhedrin court. He knew that Jesus was no ordinary man, but he was unsure what to make of him. Little did Nicodemus know of the transcendent nature of this conversation. It would provide not only for him, but the entire world, in all generations, the most insightful way to understand our relationship with God.

**Ask the "W" questions (see page 12) and identify the analogies: similarities made to convey a point.**

**You Must Be Born Again**

**JOHN 3** ¹ Now there was a man of the Pharisees named Nicodemus, a ruler of the Jews. ² This man came to Jesus by night and said to him, "Rabbi, we know that you are a teacher come from God, for no one can do these signs that you do unless God is with him."

³ Jesus answered him, "Truly, truly, I say to you, unless one is born again he cannot see the kingdom of God."

⁴ Nicodemus said to him, "How can a man be born when he is old? Can he enter a second time into his mother's womb and be born?"

⁵ Jesus answered, "Truly, truly, I say to you, unless one is born of water and the Spirit, he cannot enter the kingdom of God. ⁶ That which is born of the flesh is flesh, and that which is born of the Spirit is spirit. ⁷ Do not marvel that I said to you, 'You must be born again.' ⁸ The wind blows where it wishes, and you hear its sound, but you do not know where it comes from or where it goes. So it is with everyone who is born of the Spirit."

⁹ Nicodemus said to him, "How can these things be?"

¹⁰ Jesus answered him, "Are you the teacher of Israel and yet you do not understand these things? ¹¹ Truly, truly, I say to you, we speak of what we know, and bear witness to what we have seen, but you do not receive our testimony. ¹² If I have told you earthly things and you do not believe, how can you believe if I tell you heavenly things? ¹³ No one has ascended into heaven except he who descended from heaven, the Son of Man. ¹⁴ And as Moses lifted up the serpent in the wilderness, so must the Son of Man be lifted up, ¹⁵ that whoever believes in him may have eternal life.

## For God So Loved the World

16 "For God so loved the world, that he gave his Son, that whoever believes in him should not perish but have eternal life. 17 For God did not send his Son into the world to condemn the world, but in order that the world might be saved through him. 18 Whoever believes in him is not condemned, but whoever does not believe is condemned already, because he has not believed in the name of the only Son of God. 19 And this is the judgment: the light has come into the world, and people loved the darkness rather than the light because their works were evil. 20 For everyone who does wicked things hates the light and does not come to the light, lest his works should be exposed. 21 But whoever does what is true comes to the light, so that it may be clearly seen that his works have been carried out in God."

**4.** Even though very familiar with the Old Testament, and though he knew of Jesus' miracles (v. 2), Nicodemus is baffled by Jesus. *What about Jesus' message is difficult for him?*

**5.** The term "born again" describes the transformation Nicodemus has not yet experienced, but very much needs. *What is the point of this analogy?*

**6.** What does Jesus say are the results for those who are "born again," and for those who are not?

**7.** How does the new birth analogy contradict the idea that you can obtain God's approval through your religious performance?

**8.** "Whoever" is used five times in vv. 15-21. *In what ways does God invite us to be included in his love, his light, and his life?*

| RELATE | How It Applies to God, Life, and You > Discuss |

**9.** Jesus turns every world religious system on its head, including Nicodemus', by insisting that God's love is unearned. That love is freely given but can only be experienced by faith in him. *In what ways has God opened, or is opening your eyes to this truth?*

**10.** According to Jesus, God's healing from sin is a freely given gift. *What about that truth is difficult for you?*

*... appealing to you?*

**T-Shirt Design** After watching > discovering > relating, what slogan would you write or draw on your T-Shirt?

Wrap up by sharing with your group.

Draft concepts/quotations for summarizing this study:

Final design:

## Notes on Study #8 — Commentary and Historical Context

**NUMBERS 21:4-9—The Bronze Serpent**

- Complaining to God is not condemned in Scripture; it's celebrated. In the Psalms, we see testy, honest exchanges where David calls God to account. The Israelites had seen God's miraculous redemption in the plagues, pillar of fire, and manna from heaven. But they went beyond *complaining* to *condemning.* To speak "against God and against Moses" went too far. Hence, the Jewish people experienced God's punishment, but he also provides for their redemption. All they need to do is "look up."

- Going deeper, Numbers 21:4-9 acts as a bridge between Genesis 3:15 and John 3:14-15. Genesis 3:15 describes the snake bite which bruises the heel of God's Messiah-Redeemer (who then crushes the snake's head). John identifies the snake on the pole as Jesus' act of *crushing the biting snakes' heads* (John 3:14-15)—an act ending with his death and resurrection and the redemption of his people.

**JOHN 3:1-15—You Must Be Born Again**

- Whether to avoid the crowds and distractions, or the midday heat, or to keep his reputation intact, Nicodemus meets Jesus at night.

- Jesus cuts to the chase, confronting Nicodemus (and us) about the need for a relationship with God based on a new, born again nature. Opinions vary concerning what is meant by "born of water," but this statement parallels a natural, fleshly birth. A spiritual rebirth is likened to the wind: invisible but undeniable in its effects. Jesus' statement confronts anyone who thinks they can earn or merit the new birth through their own worthiness. Such a gift is to be *marveled in*—not so much to *marvel at* (v. 7).

**JOHN 3:16-21—For God So Loved the World**

- The leaders of Israel expect the Messiah to deal with the Romans, but Jesus would deal with sin and its tragic consequences. Sin destroys lives by separating us from God, from each other, and even from our very selves. Jesus succinctly lays out his place in God's plan, a plan that flows from one magnificent source: "For God so loved."

Study #8, Invitations | 121

 That's plausible but did it happen?

**Did Quintus express concern to Nicodemus about Jesus?** There is no "Quintus" identified in the Bible, although there are Roman magistrates and centurions like him. The Gospels do identify plenty of political tension during the time of Jesus' ministry, but no such dialogue with Nicodemus.

**Was Matthew rejected by his parents?**
The Gospels do not comment on Matthew's parents or their attitude toward him, but the portrayal of him as a traitor is how fellow Jews and his family would have viewed him.

**Did Nicodemus himself eventually become "born again"?**
Yes, that seems likely, as we see Nicodemus unashamedly identifying with Jesus again, later in the Gospel of John (7:45-52; 19:38-42).

**Did Matthew leave immediately when Jesus said, "Follow me"?**
Matthew (9:9), Mark (2:14), and Luke (5:27-28) tell us that Matthew left everything. *The Chosen* portrays the drama of his readiness in that moment! What led up to his *immediate decision* is not identified.

**Did Simon initially reject the idea of Matthew joining their group?**
We have no record of this. But "antiestablishment" types, such as fisherman Simon, and "establishment" types, such as tax collector Matthew, were bound to be at odds. They would have been all the more so as Matthew was considered a traitor to the Jewish nation.

Jesus knew that learning to value and care for each other would help prepare the disciples to minister to the diverse people they would meet. It's like he planned on calling 12 *mismatched* disciples! *The Chosen* and the Gospels increasingly portray differences over issues that brought conflict between the disciples. What they had in common was their relationship to Jesus. Sounds similar to us!

**Drive it Home** Review and Respond: Worship, Pray, Share

Watch the filmmaking process and then the finished product depicting Nicodemus' life-changing encounter with Jesus, and its meaning to you.

*Bringing John 3:16 to Screen* –Dallas Jenkins
**Type in URL:** tinyurl.com/filming-john3 (5:46 min.)

*The Chosen's Portrayal of John 3:16 (the final cut)*
**Type in URL:** tinyurl.com/God-loves-the-world (10:26 min.)

*Child of God* –We The Kingdom
**Type in URL:** tinyurl.com/child-of-God (4:31 min.)

**11.** *What are your impressions about Jesus from his conversation with Nicodemus?*

**12.** John 3:16 is probably the most well-known verse in the Bible. *What does John 3:16 mean to you personally?*

**Video Insights** Jesus as a Serpent? Numbers 21 -Mike Winger
**Type in URL:** tinyurl.com/Jesus-as-a-serpent (45:38 min.)
**Thoughts:**




You Must Be Born Again   -Tim Keller
**Type in URL:** tinyurl.com/born-again (53:18 min.)
**Thoughts:**




Seven Things You Don't Know about Matthew
**Type in URL:** tinyurl.com/about-matthew (21:46 min.) -Brandon Robbins
**Thoughts:**

## A. C. T. S. Prayer:
Adoration / Confession / Thanksgiving / Supplication

Examine where you are with the Lord and the priorities of his kingdom. Take it to him in prayer:

ADORATION: How can you praise God from whom all blessings flow?




CONFESSION: What do you need to confess and change?




THANKSGIVING: Which circumstances will you thankfully embrace?




SUPPLICATION: For whom and for what will you pray?




. . . ANYTHING ELSE:

Study #8, Invitations | 125

**S. H. A. R. E.** Mentality:
Stop / Hear / Analyze / Risk / Execute

Apply what you are learning to your opportunities, then take bold action to serve. What is a situation that you want or need to:

STOP: Take a moment to get focused. What is the issue to address?

HEAR: Listen not to the urgent, but the important. What is that?

ANALYZE: Determine the obstacles and options. How will you proceed?

RISK: Resist the familiar and easy. What's your growing edge here?

EXECUTE: Move from the mental to the real. What will you do next?

### What is your favorite Chosen episode so far?

**NOTE FOR EVERYONE:** Of course, there's a wide difference of opinion regarding the above question, but a good many will pick this final episode.

At some point it would prove fun to take a vote... and then to have group members describe why they choose the one they did. But again, if you vote before seeing this last episode—the one that the guide cover envisions—you may be sorry!

# I Am He (Episode 8)

**INTRO**: Jesus had the uncomfortable propensity to associate with the wrong kind of people. For example, he attended a dinner party at Matthew's (a "tax collector's and sinner's") house, and he engaged in conversation with an outcast woman from Samaria.

The next study (#10) will focus on the conversation Jesus has when the disciples return with food from Sychar (John 4:27-39). In this study, we will focus on Jesus' longest recorded conversation (4:1-26). And do note, the issue was not about her sin, but about her thirst.

*Identify who is involved and what contrasts are made between them.*

## DISCOVER  Read Aloud > Mark It Up > Discuss

### Jesus Calls Matthew

**Matthew 9** ⁹ As Jesus passed on from there, he saw a man called Matthew sitting at the tax booth, and he said to him, "Follow me." And he rose and followed him.

¹⁰ And as Jesus reclined at table in the house, behold, many tax collectors and sinners came and were reclining with Jesus and his disciples.

¹¹ And when the Pharisees saw this, they said to his disciples, "Why does your teacher eat with tax collectors and sinners?"

¹² But when he heard it, he said, "Those who are well have no need of a physician, but those who are sick. ¹³ Go and learn what this means: 'I desire mercy, and not sacrifice.' For I came not to call the righteous, but sinners."

1. *What is surprising about Jesus eating dinner with Matthew's friends?*

2. *Why do you think tax collectors and sinners are drawn to Jesus?*

## WATCH  View Episode 8 (51 min., from 2:01 to 52:41) > Discuss

This *Chosen* episode begins and ends at the same well, one which can be visited even today. It starts with a flashback to **Jacob and sons** digging and visited by a cynical neighbor. Jacob's twelve sons head up the original twelve tribes of Israel.

3. A major theme in this episode is being seen. *Who needs to be seen and how does Jesus assure them that they are being seen?*

4. How would you compare the priorities of Nicodemus and Zohara with those of Simon and Eden, at this point?

| DISCOVER | Read Aloud > Mark It Up > Discuss |

The Jews, who considered Samaritans as half-breeds and religious inferiors, normally bypassed Samaria when traveling between Judea and Galilee. Not Jesus. (See p. 133 for reasons why.)

**Look for and mark references to water and worship.**

**Jesus and the Samaritan Woman**
**JOHN 4** ¹ Now when Jesus learned that the Pharisees had heard that he was making and baptizing more disciples than John ² (though Jesus himself did not baptize, but only his disciples), ³ he left Judea and departed again for Galilee.

⁴ And he had to pass through Samaria. ⁵ So he came to a town of Samaria called Sychar, near the field that Jacob had given to his son Joseph. ⁶ Jacob's well was there; so Jesus, wearied as he was from his journey, was sitting beside the well. It was about the sixth hour.

⁷ A woman from Samaria came to draw water. Jesus said to her, "Give me a drink." ⁸ (For his disciples had gone away into the city to buy food.)

⁹ The Samaritan woman said to him, "How is it that you, a Jew, ask for a drink from me, a woman of Samaria?" (For Jews have no dealings with Samaritans.)

¹⁰ Jesus answered her, "If you knew the gift of God, and who it is that is saying to you, 'Give me a drink,' you would have asked him, and he would have given you living water."

¹¹ The woman said to him, "Sir, you have nothing to draw water with, and the well is deep. Where do you get that living water? ¹² Are you greater than our father Jacob? He gave us the well and drank from it himself, as did his sons and his livestock."

¹³ Jesus said to her, "Everyone who drinks of this water will be thirsty again, ¹⁴ but whoever drinks of the water that I will give him will never be thirsty again. The water that I will give him will become in him a spring of water welling up to eternal life."

¹⁵ The woman said "Sir, give me this water, so that I will not be thirsty or have to come here to draw water."

¹⁶ Jesus said to her, "Go, call your husband, and then come here."

¹⁷ The woman answered him, "I have no husband."

Jesus said to her, "You are right in saying, 'I have no husband'; ¹⁸ for you have had five husbands, and the one you now have is not really your husband. What you have said is true."

¹⁹ The woman responded to him, "Sir, I perceive that you are a prophet. ²⁰ Our fathers worshiped on this mountain, but you say that in Jerusalem is the place where people ought to worship."

*Study #9, I Am He* | **131**

²¹ Jesus said to her, "Woman, believe me, the hour is coming when neither on this mountain nor in Jerusalem will you worship the Father. ²² You worship what you do not know; we worship what we know, for salvation is from the Jews. ²³ But the hour is coming, and is now here, when the true worshipers will worship the Father in spirit and truth, for the Father is seeking such people to worship him. ²⁴ God is spirit, and those who worship him must worship in spirit and truth."

²⁵ The woman said to him, "I know that the Messiah is coming (he who is called Christ). When he comes, he will tell us all things."

²⁶ Jesus said to her, "I who speak to you am he."

**5.** *What barriers (geographical, political, theological, social, gender) does Jesus break down by entering a conversation with the woman?*

**6.** *How does Jesus lead to the point of revealing his identity?*

**7.** *What does Jesus want to teach her about true worship?*

**RELATE** How It Applies to God, Life, and You > Discuss

**8.** *Describe the first time you felt a thirst for what Jesus has to offer.*

132 | The Chosen Study, Season One

**9.** What was it that opened your eyes to who Jesus is?

**T-Shirt Design** After watching > discovering > relating, What slogan would you write or draw on your T-Shirt?

**Draft concepts:**

**Final design:**

## Notes on Study #9 — Commentary and Historical Context

**John 4:1-30—Having our Thirst Quenched**

- Samaritans' and Jews' animosity toward each other can be traced back to the Assyrian invasion of Northern Israel in 721 AD. The conquerors took many Samaritan Jews into captivity. Foreigners repopulated and intermarried, altering the inhabitants' Judaism with other religious rites, even paganism (see 2 Kings 17:24-29).

  When Zerubbabel returned from exile to rebuild Jerusalem's temple, (between 538 and 520 BC), he spurned Samaritan help. Given their very different religious orientation, the Samaritans then sought to prevent the Temple from being rebuilt (Ezra 4:1-10). They built their own temple on Mt. Gerizim, which was later destroyed by the Jews.

- Jesus is the master conversationalist. He breaks down conventions (male vs. female, Jew vs. Samaritan, rabbi vs. sinner), builds common ground, avoids diversion, and gets to the woman's real need. This conversation is a great example of how to build rapport, identify a person's need, and seek to meet it in a meaningful way.

- This woman is an outcast (comes to the well alone at noon, has had five husbands) and suffered much rejection. Jesus offers her *living water* to meet her deepest need—a relationship with himself. Jesus' offer is as radical as *living water* is to well water (see John 7:37-39).

*That's plausible but did it happen?*

**Did Jacob dig a well that Jesus visited (and that still exists today)?** Although there is no specific record of Jacob and sons digging a well, he came to Shechem, which is called Sychar in John 4, where he pitched a tent and built an altar (Genesis 33:18-20). The well in John 4 is called "Jacob's well," and tradition identifies him as having dug it.

**Was Simon Peter the only married disciple?** Yes, as far as we know. Although it would be interesting to know about Simon's wife and their relationship as the show speculates, we have no biblical account beyond the fact that he had a mother-in-law and, thus, a wife!

## Drive it Home | Review and Respond: Worship, Pray, Share

Rewatch the encounter between Jesus and the woman put to song. Consider Jesus' grace in reaching out to this woman and... to you.

**The Woman at the Well:** *-Olivia Wilde*
**Type in URL:** tinyurl.com/woman-at-the-well-song (4:26 min.)

*I Just Need You* -TobyMac
**Type in URL:** tinyurl.com/I-just-need-you (3:56 min.)

**10.** *How do people today seek to quench their spiritual thirst, find hope and a sense of purpose?*

**11.** A recurring theme has been people finding their needs met by Jesus—"Water for the Thirsty." *When you consider your greatest needs, what comes to mind?*

**12.** *In what ways has Jesus met your needs for hope and purpose in life? (Or how have you considered trusting him to do so?)*

**Study #9, I Am He | 135**

**Video Insights** The Chosen in Israel, Samaritan scene
**Type in URL:** tinyurl.com/woman-at-the-well  -Dallas Jenkins
**Thoughts:**                               (6:25 min.)

The Woman at the Well -Janet Parshall
**Type in URL:** tinyurl.com/living-water-life (57:36 min.)
**Thoughts:**

Woman at the Well -Brenda Salter McNeil
**Type in URL:** tinyurl.com/living-water-lifestyle (40:02 min.)
**Thoughts:**

## A. C. T. S. Prayer:
Adoration / Confession / Thanksgiving / Supplication

Examine where you are with the Lord and the priorities of his kingdom. Take it to him in prayer:

ADORATION: How can you praise God from whom all blessings flow?




CONFESSION: What do you need to confess and change?




THANKSGIVING: Which circumstances will you thankfully embrace?




SUPPLICATION: For whom and for what will you pray?




. . . ANYTHING ELSE:

**S. H. A. R. E.** Mentality:
Stop / Hear / Analyze / Risk / Execute

Apply what you are learning to your opportunities, then take bold action to serve. What is a situation that you want or need to:

STOP: Take a moment to get focused. What is the issue to address?

HEAR: Listen not to the urgent, but the important. What is that?

ANALYZE: Determine the obstacles and options. How will you proceed?

RISK: Resist the familiar and easy. What's your growing edge here?

EXECUTE: Move from the mental to the real. What will you do next?

A Possible 11th Study: Pages 150-158

**NOTE FOR LEADERS:** Upcoming is the 10th study and there is one more... or maybe two if you'd like! You could plan for an *11th Study Overview and Wrap-Up*. Here are three options:

1) Your group could meet at its **normal time and do its usual study**. In this case, you would use pages 150-156 to guide the 11th study called "Your Faith Journey."

2) As an alternative, your group could schedule an **all-day event**,* perhaps a Saturday gathering—maybe at a different location, and extend the "Your Faith Journey" interaction together.

3) Or your group could extend the study further as a **weekend retreat*** to include even more time for study, prayer, quiet time, and fun!

One way or another, think through how to make your last gathering special and a time that provides momentum for your next study!

*For more input on creating longer events, see **Leaders** on the website.

# Integrate Your Chosen Experience
### Season One Reviewed and Looking Ahead

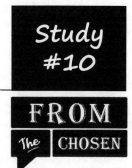

**INTRO:** The cover on this guide illustrates the centrality of water in our lives. But of course, our thirst runs deeper. We have a "God-shaped void" only God himself can satisfy.

Jesus works hard to get his point across to the woman he meets at the well, later identified as **Photina**. He tells her that the source to quench such thirst comes only from a relationship with him. He will be her Messiah—the anointed, Servant-King, sent from God the Father.

Let's see how "water of life" carries through as a biblical theme. We can trace this source of life from Creation to this very encounter at Jacob's Well.

**WATCH** View BibleProject.com, Water of Life (4 min.) > Discuss
(tinyurl.com/water-of-life)

This video depicts the "water of life" image in the following scenes:

... the river in the Garden of Eden (Gen 2:5-6)
... the drought of the human condition
... Jacob digs a well, restarting God's family
... the desert, dry bones and thirst continue
... the "woman at the well" story reimagined
... Jesus' death on the cross as a fountain
... the climax of God's Spirit in us bringing life

**1.** When have you felt spiritually or emotionally "thirsty" (far from God, alone, betrayed, outcast)?

**2.** How has or could the "water of life," described in this video, impact your life?

**REWATCH** View Episode 8 (15 min. from 0:00 to 4:26 and from 40:08 to 50:48) > Discuss

**3.** Let's revisit the *living water* scene from this story. Even though the woman leaves her water jug at the well, she is no longer thirsty. How has Jesus satisfied her deepest needs?

**4.** While she came to the well as a woman of shame, she leaves as an emissary of restoration. *How do you imagine this turn of events will impact the woman and others in her hometown of Sychar?*

---

**DISCOVER** Read Aloud > Mark It Up > Discuss

**INTRO:** The disciples, having gone to town to find food, now return and offer some to Jesus. His response leaves them even more confused. Apparently, he is getting his hunger satisfied with something else, and he wants them to have the same experience.

**Look for the priorities and how they're expressed by each character.**

**The Disciples Return**

**JOHN 4** [27] Just then his disciples came back. They marveled that he was talking with a woman, but no one said, "What do you seek?" or, "Why are you talking with her?"

[28] So the woman left her water jar and went into town and said to the people, [29] "Come, see a man who told me all that I ever did. Can this be the Christ?" [30] They went out of the town and were coming to him.

[31] Meanwhile the disciples were urging him, saying, "Rabbi, eat."

[32] But he said, "I have food to eat that you do not know about."

[33] So the disciples said to one another, "Has anyone brought him something to eat?"

[34] Jesus said to them, "My food is to do the will of him who sent me and to accomplish his work. [35] Do you not say, 'There are yet four months, then comes the harvest'? Look, I tell you, lift up your eyes.

See that the fields are white for harvest. ³⁶ Already the one who reaps is receiving wages and gathering fruit for eternal life, so that sower and reaper may rejoice together. ³⁷ For here the saying holds true, 'One sows and another reaps.' ³⁸ I sent you to reap that for which you did not labor. Others have labored, and you have entered into their labor." ³⁹ Many Samaritans from that town believed in him because of the woman's testimony, "He told me all that I ever did."

⁴⁰ So when the Samaritans came to him, they asked him to stay with them, and he stayed there two days. ⁴¹ And many more believed because of his word. ⁴² They said to the woman, "It is no longer because of what you said that we believe, for we have heard for ourselves, and we know that this is indeed the Savior of the world."

**5.** *What do the disciples find confusing about Jesus' words and actions?*

**6.** *What is the "living food" that Jesus is talking about and wants his disciples to have?*

**7.** *Compared to the expected harvest four months away, what kind of harvest timeframe does Jesus envision for him and his disciples?*

# Study #10, Integrate Your Chosen Experience | 143

**RELATE** How It Applies to God, Life, and You > Discuss

Jesus uses many metaphors in this passage. He enjoys *living food* as he provides *living water* to the woman and, through her, to her village. He then invites his disciples to participate with him in a *living harvest*.

8. In John 4:34 Jesus said, "My food is to do the will of him who sent me and to accomplish his work." *How does his mission statement challenge you to rearrange priorities?*

9. *What kind of "life-sustaining work" is he directing you to do?*

10. *Where would you have placed yourself on this continuum (put a smaller x) regarding your relationship with God/Jesus when you began this study (see p. 44)? Where are you now (put a larger X)?*

   ---

   Observer...    Skeptic...    Learner...    Seeker...    Follower...

11. *In your overall study, what new spiritual perspective do you have about* God/Jesus?

   ... direction in your life?

**T-Shirt Design** After watching > discovering > relating, what slogan would you write or draw on your T-Shirt? Wrap up by sharing with your group.

Draft concepts/quotations for summarizing this study:

Final design:

# Notes on Study #10 — Commentary and Historical Context

## John 4:31-39—The Disciples Return

- Like *living water* that replenishes the spirit, there is *living food* that sustains the soul. The disciples completely miss the point in their focus on ordinary food, wondering if Jesus had already eaten.

- Many pursuits energize us. For Jesus, it is God's work in the lives of people that provides real satisfaction—forsaking small ambitions for the larger ambition of meeting people's deepest needs.

- Jesus' "food" comes in providing *living water* through the woman's word. This event lays the groundwork for a *living harvest* among the Samaritans, coming in Season Two. Check out John 4:39-42.

## The Fish Symbolism

It's hard not to notice all the references to fish in *The Chosen*, especially in the opening credits of each episode. Here we see fish swimming in one direction as some reverse course in the other—an obvious reference to the change Jesus brings into a person's life.

After the Cross, the fish is the most prominent image of Christianity. Early Christians used it as in art and, in times of persecution, it may have come in handy as a kind of code—drawing half of the image in the sand when meeting a stranger to see if he or she drew the other half and thus identified as a fellow believer. (Spoiler alert for Christmas Special called *The Messengers*. See page 182.)

The word "fish" in Greek is ΙΧΘΥΣ (ICHTHYS in English). Each Greek letter was given a unique value: *Ἰησοῦς Χριστός, Θεοῦ Υἱός, Σωτήρ* or Jesus, Christ, God('s), Son, Savior

The Greek word for fish, pronounced I-CH-TH-Y-S

First letters = Jesus, Christ, God('s), Son, Savior

## Drive it Home — Review and Respond: Worship, Pray, Share

Watch, listen, and even sing this hymn written in 1757, as an expression of your desire for Jesus' work of grace to enter deeply into your life.

*Come Thou Fount* – Celtic Worship
**Type in URL:** tinyurl.com/come-thou (5:06 min.)

*Do It Again* – Elevation Worship
**Type in URL:** tinyurl.com/do-it-again (10:14 min.)

**8.** *What is difficult for you in contemplating Jesus' invitation to become not just a Sower, but a Harvester of people as well?*

**9.** *Which friends, neighbors, co-workers, and/or family members do you sense God would have you help (as a seed Sower) through service, prayer, and dialogue about spiritual things? Identify them:*

- 
- 
- 

- 
- 
- 

- 
- 
- 

**14.** *What can you imagine this will involve?*

*… What are your next steps? (Including prayer.)*

**Video Insights** *Season Finale: What You Probably Didn't Notice*
**Type in URL:** tinyurl.com/episode8-explained  –Brandon Robbins
**Thoughts:**                                 (29:36 min.)
___

*Living Water, Pt. 1, 2 and 3* –John MacArthur
**Type in URL:** tinyurl.com/living-water-part1 (55:47 min)
**Type in URL:** tinyurl.com/living-water-part2 (53:43 min.)
**Type in URL:** tinyurl.com/living-water-part3 (56:57 min.)
**Thoughts:**
___

**A. C. T. S.** Prayer:

Adoration / Confession / Thanksgiving / Supplication

Examine where you are with the Lord and the priorities of his kingdom. Take it to him in prayer:

ADORATION: How can you praise God from whom all blessings flow?



CONFESSION: What do you need to confess and change?



THANKSGIVING: Which circumstances will you thankfully embrace?



SUPPLICATION: For whom and for what will you pray?



... ANYTHING ELSE:

Study #10, Integrate Your Chosen Experience | 149

## S. H. A. R. E. Mentality:
### Stop / Hear / Analyze / Risk / Execute

Apply what you are learning to your opportunities, then take bold action to serve. What is a situation that you want or need to:

STOP: Take a moment to get focused. What is the issue to address?

HEAR: Listen not to the urgent, but the important. What is that?

ANALYZE: Determine the obstacles and options. How will you proceed?

RISK: Resist the familiar and easy. What's your growing edge here?

EXECUTE: Move from the mental to the real. What will you do next?

| Your Faith Journey | Extend Your Drive it Home Session

What follows provides a *look back* to Season One's study and a *look forward* to your life-experience. Use these questions to extend your personal *Drive it Home* reflection time or schedule another time to complete this. *When can you do so?* _____

**15.** First, read through pages 157-163 which describe the Gospels' characters and authors—their identity and calling. Also, for added input, look up the following link: jesusstudy.org/his-disciples

*What has encouraged, challenged or surprised you about their stories?*

*Next, describe your "big picture" takeaway from the study here and on pages 151-155 and yes, end with a T-Shirt!*

# Your Faith Journey | 151

**Review the studies. What are your takeaways from each?**

**Study #1, The Shepherd,** Pilot Episode (pp. 21-35):
   Micah 5:2-5; Is. 9:2-7, 35:3-6, 7:14; Luke 2:1-21

**Study #2, I Have Called You by Name,** Episode 1 (pp. 37-47):
   Luke 7:36-50

**Study #3, Shabbat,** Episode 2 (pp. 49-61):
   Genesis 1:1-2:3; Exodus 20:8-11

**Study #4, Jesus Loves the Little Children,** Episode 3 (pp. 63-73):
   Matthew: 19:13-15; 18:1-6

**Study #5, The Rock on Which it is Built,** Episode 4 (pp. 75-85):
   Luke 4:38-5:11

## More takeaways?

**Study #6, The Wedding Gift,** Episode 5 (pp. 87-99): Luke 2:40-52; John 2:1-12

**Study #7, Indescribable Compassion,** Episode 6 (pp. 101-111): Isaiah 40:3-5; Mark 1:40-2:12

**Study #8, Invitations,** Episode 7 (pp. 113-125): Numbers 21:4-9; John 3:1-21

**Study #9, I Am He,** Episode 8, (pp. 127-137): Matthew 9:9-13; John 4:1-26

**Study #10, Integrate Your Chosen Experience,** Episode 8B (pp. 139-149): John 4:27-39; Review; Looking Ahead

> **WRAP-UP** Read this definition of faith. Spend some time to mark-it-up (and share with others).

*The Chosen is meant to take you into the eyes and ears of the people who followed Jesus. We believe that if you can see Jesus through the eyes of those who met him, you can be changed and impacted in the same way they were.... If we can connect you with their burdens and struggles and questions, then ideally, we can connect you to the solution, to the answer to those questions.* —Dallas Jenkins

One definition of genuine faith is *giving all you know about yourself to all you know about God.* Such is the call to humility. The more you hang around Jesus, the more you realize that he isn't impressed with pretension. Maybe that's why he—the Servant-King, God's understated Messiah—made no grand entry. Instead, Jesus shows up as a baby, born in a dirty stable to a peasant girl, in a nondescript town.

30 years later, for three short years, he announces that the Kingdom of God has arrived, complete with spiritually intriguing stories and miracles. He offers forgiveness of sin, and reconciliation to God the Father—all culminating in his crucifixion, resurrection, and ascension.

Something is going on here. No one could make this stuff up. If nothing more, **the story of Jesus is the most [ _____ fill in the blank] story that humanity has to offer**. The Gospel writers certainly felt this way and their eagerness to describe this off-the-charts, unusual *eternity-meets-time event* pours through their accounts.

*From your study,* **write in the adjective** *that best describes Jesus' story:*
    Remarkable...
        Compelling...
            Audacious...
                Captivating...
Negative ones are fair game.      Fascinating...
**Hey, we chose one—what's yours?**    Intriguing...
Share why you selected it with your group.    Other...

I've discovered the most _____ story ever told.

## Final questions for contemplation (and sharing with others)

*Do you increasingly find yourself caught up in Jesus' story, as well? Do you want it, and him, to influence your life more deeply? Then, take on what you learn. If Jesus says to love your enemies, try it out. Or, if he says to show hospitality like the Good Samaritan, or to help find lost sheep like a Good Shepherd, then do it.*

*As you "try on Jesus' teaching," you will find it not only making sense, but that you will also need to look to him for the wisdom, strength, and courage to take the risk of making some hard choices. Thankfully, in this journey of faith, his forgiveness is always close at hand.*

*How have you connected with the above quote by Dallas?*

*How do you respond to the definition of faith given on page 153?*

*Which teaching of Jesus would God have you "try on" right now?*

*With whom can you share what you've learned and its impact on you?*

Your Faith Journey | 155

**T-Shirt Design** As you look back over the entire season, what slogan would you write or draw on your T-Shirt? Wrap up by sharing with others.

Draft concepts/quotations for the OVERALL SEASON:

Final design:

**Your Faith Journey** (for additional space, see page 190 ff.):

## Background Notes | The Four Gospels*

Early tradition identifies Matthew, Mark, Luke, and John as the ones who introduced Jesus to the First Century world and to ours. Their portrait of him is both historically unique and remarkably consistent.

**MATTHEW:** Given his occupation as a tax collector for the Roman government, we can only imagine the initial tension between Matthew (also called Levi) and the other disciples. But reconciliation lay at the heart of Jesus' message (see *The Sermon on the Mount,* Mathew 5-7). Matthew's Gospel emphasizes the interconnectedness between the Old and New Testaments and provides young believers a systematic tutorial on Jesus' teaching which is why it was put first in the NT.

**MARK:** This Gospel has been generally recognized as the account coming from Peter. Mark begins his first "sentence" with no verb: *The beginning of the Gospel about Jesus Christ, the Son of God*. His last sentence ends with the women fleeing Jesus' empty tomb *because they were afraid*. For Mark, Jesus is a man of action. To help believers facing persecution from the Roman state, Mark focuses on Jesus as the Suffering Servant who "came to serve" (Mark 10:45).

**LUKE:** An educated Greek physician and traveling companion of Paul, Luke authored the book of Acts and the Gospel that bears his name. Although Luke never met Jesus himself, he had a close relationship with Paul, and was acquainted with most of the key eyewitnesses who knew Jesus (Luke 1:1-4). After extensive interviews with these contacts, Luke begins: "Since I myself have carefully investigated everything from the beginning, it seemed good also to me to write an orderly account" (Luke 1:3).

**JOHN:** A fisherman and brother of James, he writes, "In the beginning was the Word," offering a rather obvious parallel to the opening words of Genesis. In the "first Genesis," God spoke *Creation* into existence, and in the "second Genesis" God speaks *Redemption* into existence: "The Word became flesh and made his dwelling among us" (1:14). This "Word made flesh" is who John wants his readers to know.

*The Gospels and John: Two Quick Overviews -Whiteboard Bible Study tinyurl.com/four-gospels (10:40) / tinyurl.com/overview-john (8:01)

Mark is the shortest Gospel, likely written first (around AD 65) and orginating from the ministry of Peter. Many scholars believe Matthew and Luke had access to Mark because 76% of Mark's Gospel ends up in both Matthew and Luke and **97% of his Gospel ends up one or the other of them**. These three Synoptics (similar summaries) borrow from each and other independent sources as this chart suggests.

The content in **John's Gospel is 92% unique**. It covers a different time span than the others; it sets much of Jesus' ministry in Judea; and it portrays him discoursing at length on theological matter (see the next page regarding John's uniqueness).

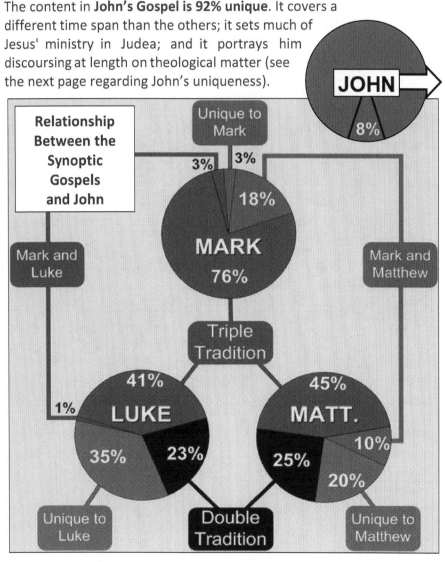

The relationship between the Synoptic Gospels chart is courtesy wikimedia.org of: tinyurl.com/between-gospels Also see the web link on page 161 for more info.

## John's Gospel provides seven signs

Of the 37 miracles recorded in the NT, John goes in-depth into seven of them to validate Jesus' Messianic claim. And, if that isn't enough to assert deity, the I AM statements, God's name first given to Moses in Exodus (see circle below), make explicit who he claims to be—God himself.

01 Turning water into wine
02 Healing the noble's son
03 Healing the man at the pool
04 Feeding the 5,000
05 Walking on water
06 Healing the man born blind
07 Raising Lazarus from the dead

## John identifies Jesus' nature as the eternal "I AM"

Jesus of Nazareth Is The Eternal **I AM**
Exodus 3:13-15; John 8:56-58

- WAY — John 14:6
- TRUTH — John 14:6
- LIFE — John 14:6
- RESURRECTION — John 11:5
- REAL VINE — John 15:1
- GOOD SHEPHERD — John 10:11
- GATE for the SHEEP — John 10:7
- LIGHT of the WORLD — John 8:12
- BREAD of LIFE — John 6:35

***History's most audacious story:*** jesusstudy.org/gospels-compared

## Comparison of the Gospels

| | MARK | MATTHEW | LUKE | JOHN |
|---|---|---|---|---|
| **Writer (Traditional)** | Companion of Peter, the John Mark from Acts | Former tax collector (Levi) and one of the twelve | A Greek physician and traveling companion of Paul | Former fisherman, one of the twelve, beloved disciple |
| **Date Written** | AD 63-70 | AD 75-80 | AD 80-85 | AD 90-100 |
| **Images of Christ** | **Man of Action** Proclaims the kingdom of God and forgiveness of sin, Son of Man and Liberator, calling followers | **Master Teacher** Visited at birth by magi, new Moses and King to restore Israel as promised Messiah, Deliverer and Son of God | **Merciful Savior** Visited at birth by shepherds. The compassionate Champion. Loves the poor, children, women, outcasts | **The God-Man** The Logos, Word of God, Creator and Light of the World, Son of God, Lamb of God, Redeemer in total control |
| **Written to:** | Romans | Jews | Greeks | Everyone |
| **The Author's Community** | Christian community in Rome undergoing persecution | Jewish Christian community in Antioch, Syria | Theophilus (*Lover of God*) possibly represents all Christians (Greece) | Community of Jews, Gentiles, and Samaritans of Ephesus In Turkey |
| **Theme: Jesus as** | **Suffering Servant** | **Messiah King** | **Redeemer** | **Son of God** |
| **General Theme** | Jesus 'takes over" from John the Baptist as the Promised One, healing, forgiving. ("immediately") | Jesus teaches what it means to be a member of the Kingdom of Heaven and a growing disciple. | Jesus finds the lost and heals divisions among people. He shows compassion for those in need of help and hope. | Jesus is God, full of grace and truth. Salvation available for those who believe and commit their lives (7 signs). |
| **Feature** | **Miracles** | **Sermons** | **Parables** | **"I AM" Statements** |
| **Historical Situation** | The Romans subdue armed Jewish rebellions, Christians are experiencing persecution. | Written after Rome had destroyed Jerusalem whose destruction was prophesied by Jesus at the Temple. | Written when the persecution of Christians was intensifying throughout the Roman Empire. | Domitian mandated that all people worship him. Jewish leaders banned Christians from synagogues. |
| **Caesars** | Nero: AD 54-68 | Vespasian and Titus: AD 70-81 | Domitian: AD 81-96 | Domitian: AD 81-96 Nerva: AD 96-98 Trajan: AD 98-117 |
| **Key Verses** | 10:45 | 16:13-20 | 19:10 | 20:30-31 |

**Note:** The link on the next page provides more background on each disciple and shows the film depiction of their calling by Jesus in *The Chosen*.

## Jesus' disciples identity and calling: jesusstudy.org/his-disciples

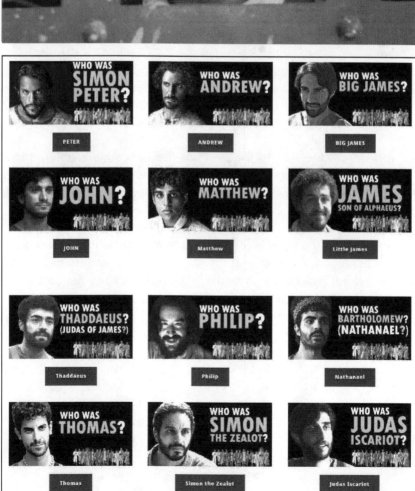

## Knowing those who knew him best

**Mary Magdalene:** She was one of several women mentioned in Luke 8:2-3, who had been "cured of evil spirits and diseases," and was following Jesus. Having been delivered from seven demons, she is with Jesus at the cross and is the first one to whom Jesus appears after the Crucifixion (Luke 8:2-3; John 19:25-27; John 20:1-18).

**Nicodemus:** As a Pharisee, he also ruled as a member of the Sanhedrin, the supreme religious council in Jerusalem during New Testament times. His encounter with Jesus in John 3 is the occasion for the well-known verse, John 3:16. He boldly steps up to help bury Jesus' body, with Joseph of Arimathea, post-crucifixion (John 3:1-21; 7:45-52; 19:38-42).

**John the Baptist:** Miraculously conceived shortly before his cousin Jesus, he heralds Jesus, as foretold by Isaiah (40:3-5), calling Jews to repent in preparation for the Messiah. After a faithful ministry, and baptizing Jesus, he is imprisoned and later beheaded for the threat he posed to Herod Antipas. Jesus identifies him as the "greatest of those born of women" (John 1:6-34; Matthew 3:1-17; 11:1-19; 14:1-12; Luke 1:5-25, 57-80).

**Andrew:** One of the first to follow Jesus, he brings his brother, Simon (Peter), right away. Together with fellow fishermen, James and John, Andrew leaves everything to follow Jesus after the miraculous catch. He also plays a key role in the feeding of the 5,000 (John 1:40-42; 6:8-9).

**Simon:** This fisherman meets Jesus and is later renamed Peter, *the Rock*. He is brought to Jesus by his brother, Andrew, and follows Jesus thereafter. He is well known for walking (and sinking) on water, slicing off a soldier's ear, denying Jesus before his death, being a prominent leader in the early Christian movement, and for writing 1 and 2 Peter (Matthew 14:25-32; 16:13-28; Mark 14:66-72; John 1:40-42; Luke 5:1-11).

**James and John:** Along with Simon, they become Jesus' closest disciples. Appropriately nicknamed by Jesus as the "sons of thunder" (Luke 9:54), they were Simon's partners and, like him, they left everything to follow Jesus after the huge catch of fish (Mark 3:17; Luke 5:1-11). John goes on to write a Gospel, three letters, and the Book of Revelation.

**Zebedee** and **Salome** are the parents of James and John. Salome is named twice in Scripture and is highlighted several other times. Though not above asking favor for her sons (Matthew 20:20-28), she is a devoted follower of Jesus. She is there at his crucifixion (Mark 15:40) and the Resurrection (Mark 16:1). (See also Matthew 20:20-28; Mark 10:35-40)

**Matthew:** Also known as Levi, he is a despised tax collector when Jesus calls him from his tax booth to follow Him. He "left everything and followed him," and invites many friends and coworkers to a dinner with Jesus (Luke 5:27-32). He authors the Gospel of Matthew.

**James the Less** (*micros,* meaning "little" or "young") and **Thaddeus**: Two lesser-known disciples. "Little James," a son of Alphaeus (Mark 3:18), could have been Matthew's brother (also a son of Alphaeus, Mark 2:14), but never identified as such. Thaddeus, aka Jude or Judas, may have gotten his nickname (meaning "breast child" or "mama's boy") to distinguish him from the other Judas, whose name carries negative connotations.

**Thomas** (aka Didymus, or "twin"): Best known for doubting: *Unless I see the nail marks in his hands... I will not believe* (John 20:25). Thomas could, maybe more accurately, be called *logical*. Regardless, we see a wholehearted passion, even an openness to die with Jesus (11:16), and fear of missing him (14:5). Thomas, the last of The Twelve to see Jesus after the Resurrection, upon seeing him proclaims, *My Lord and my God* (20:24-29).

**Mary, mother of Jesus:** She is the teenager God chose to give birth to Jesus, who was conceived in her by the Holy Spirit. She raises Jesus from birth, along with **Joseph**. Joseph marries her after an angel appears to him in a dream; he probably died before Jesus began his adult ministry. Mary weeps at the Crucifixion, witnesses the resurrected Christ and, along with at least some of her other children (Acts 1:14), is part of the early church (Luke 1:26-56; 2:5-7; 8:19-21; John 2:1-12; 19:25-27).

**The Leper:** An outcast and "untouchable" in his society (Leviticus 13:46), this particular leper receives compassion and healing from Jesus. Even Jesus touching him would have been shocking, both to him and to any onlookers. He is only the first of many lepers and other social outcasts—the paralyzed, blind, lame, sick, and demon-possessed—that Jesus heals and cleanses (Matthew 8:2-4; Mark 1:40-45; Luke 5:12-16; 17:11-19).

## Spoiler Alert! What happens next...

**Episode 1:** The opening scene not only sets the stage for Season Two, but it also serves as prologue for how the Gospels were written. Here we find **John** interviewing key witnesses, writing notes and musing with Jesus' mother, Mary, about how to begin his Gospel.

After Jesus encounters **Photina**, the Samaritan woman, he and his disciples visit her hometown of Sychar for two days (John 4:43). During this time, **James** and **John** till a field, and the disciples "lose" Jesus while he fixes a cart axle. Also, Photina's husband, among others, listens to Jesus tell the Parable of the Lost Sheep (Luke 15:1-7). The parable foreshadows a fascinating encounter with a "lost sheep," **Melech**, and an interesting reference to the Good Samaritan parable.

**Episode 2:** The disciples welcome **Philip**—a student of John the Baptist, and friend of Andrew. Now changing allegiance from John to Jesus, he seeks out his old friend, **Nathanael**, with whom he shares the good news. Nathanael (in this show, a failed architect) was despondent over a collapsed building and the loss of his career. But he finds new purpose in meeting and following the man who saw him under a fig tree.

**Episode 3:** No new characters, but crowds of people line up for healing. We listen in on compelling insights as the disciples, including Mother Mary, seek to understand the movement they have joined. Tensions rise as Simon and Andrew confront Matthew about his former life. But their arguments look petty as an exhausted Jesus returns, laboring as he walks through the camp to his tent.

**Episode 4:** Here we meet **Jesse**, permanently lame from a childhood accident until he is healed by Jesus some 38 years later (John 5:1-9). His brother in this show, **Simon the Zealot**—trained as an assassin, but stunned to see his brother healed—rejects his zealot vows to join this new movement. Jesus increasingly "stirs up the water," coming to the attention of the Roman authorities and Jewish religious leaders.

**Episode 5:** The older cousin by six months, **John the Baptist** and Jesus have a private conversation. **Mary Magdalene** struggles with PTSD from a close encounter with a Roman soldier and a demon-possessed man called **Legion** (real name, **Caleb**), who is delivered by Jesus. She ends up drawn back into her old lifestyle and leaves the group, who are all very concerned about her disappearance. Jesus sends Simon and Matthew to look for and, hopefully, return her.

**Episode 6:** Mary falls deeper into old habits, but Simon and Matthew find her and bring her back. She meets with Jesus, who is quick to extend forgiveness. The focus on love over law, and recovery over relapse, stands in sharp contrast to the views of the Pharisees, **Shmuel** and **Yanni**. They seek to bring Jesus to 'justice' for what they see as blasphemy, for healings and grain eating (harvesting) on the Sabbath.

**Episode 7:** Jesus and his disciples prepare for an upcoming sermon to be witnessed by thousands. But that scenario appears to blow up when Roman soldiers lead Jesus away to Capernaum for questioning before **Quintus** (the Roman Praetor from Season One) and one of Caesar's cohorts, **Atticus**, who has been tailing Jesus. Andrew, despondent over John's imprisonment, leaves the group along with Philip. They come upon the Egyptian woman, **Tamar**, and the healed paralytic—both speaking about Jesus while Jesus is wanted for questioning. The episode ends with Jesus returning and the disciples asking him to teach them how to pray in the same manner that he does. Their desire to get "the heart and the mind right" pleases Jesus.

**Episode 8:** We anticipate the Big Reveal, as Jesus and Matthew work together on what will be called the *Sermon on the Mount* (Matthew 5-7). Jesus comes up with just the right introduction (the Beatitudes), while the disciples busy themselves with finding and negotiating the right spot, preparing leaflets, inviting townsfolk, welcoming old friends, and parents—plus crowd control. Thousands gather, including one who finds himself caught up in it all, **Judas (Iscariot)**. Jesus, decked out in a blue "Prince of Peace" sash, finally takes to the stage, and... (hold the drum roll, please) the long awaited Big Reveal will now be... delivered in Season Three.

## MARK where it happened on the map

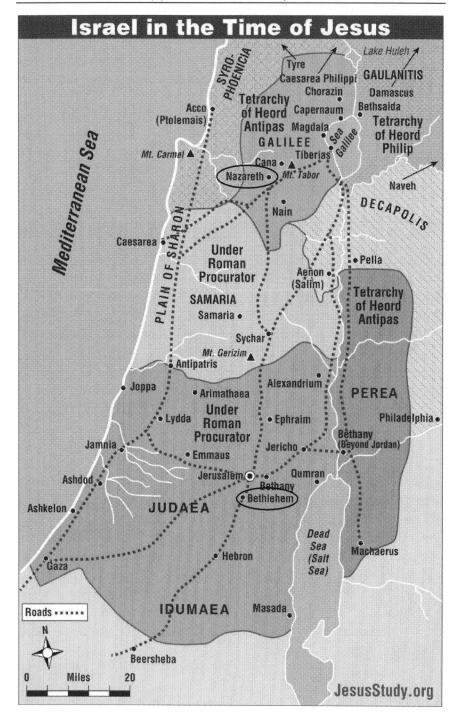

RECORD locations cited and what happened there:

- Bethlehem Ephrathah: Micah 5:2 (p. 22) Jesus' birthplace
- Nazareth, Jesus' hometown: Luke 2:4 (p. 26)
- Bethlehem (City of David): Luke 2:4, 15 (p. 26)
-
-
-
-

**Note:** For printable maps, see: jesusstudy.org/maps-from-jesus-time

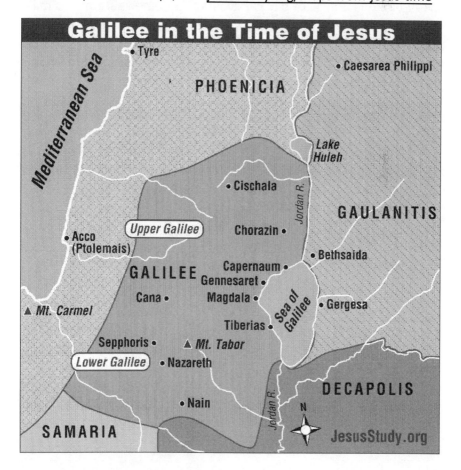

## Can you trust The Chosen?

Some have raised questions about the authenticity of *The Chosen*—which is what this guide's *Realistic But Real?* sections highlight. An analogy to Bible translation could be made in this regard.

Bible translations fall into three general categories: 1) *word-for-word*, strictly following the original Hebrew and Greek, 2) *thought-for-thought*, which reworks sentence structures to better fit the native language, and 3) *paraphrase*, an even looser translation of the original.

A few other "translations" go even further and *amplify* the original meaning to give readers more historical and literary context with which they may be unfamiliar.

Every film enactment of biblical events falls somewhere on a similar spectrum: from a literal *word-for-word* depiction, to a *thought-for-thought*, to a *paraphrase*. In the case of *The Chosen*, it would be fair to characterize it as *beyond paraphrase* to an "amplified version." Some would use this byline under it: *Based on a True Story*.

Such use of "non-literal," *historical fiction* relies on artistic license, and can cause discomfort which is understandable. If that is true for you, check out the videos by Dallas entitled: *Can you trust The Chosen?* (tinyurl.com/trusting-the-chosen), as well as his interview with Jonathan Roumie, (tinyurl.com/roumie-interview), who portrays Jesus. These videos convey their perspective and may prove helpful.

We regularly point out what happened versus plausible speculation from *The Chosen*. Ultimately, *The Chosen* is a TV show, and the Bible is the only media inspired by God, given to inform us of the truth and the way things happened. Film brings supportive context and three-dimensional color to the two-dimensional writing on the page.

Dallas' heartfelt, well-conceived mission (see page 15) is why we vigorously support *The Chosen* and have developed *The Chosen Study*.

## Leader's Notes

**The Chosen Vision:** Dallas and his team share the goal of *reaching a billion people with the message of Jesus*. Our "loaves and fish" effort joins their far-reaching aspirations by **helping study leaders** facilitate discussions about Jesus with everyone we know, and to see people grow into and as Christ followers.

If you're on the fence about leading, consider Jesus' challenge to Andrew in Episode 8 of Season One about traveling through the hated Samaritan territory, a place considered unclean and dangerous: *Did you join me for safety reasons?*

**So, you're interested in leading a Chosen Study? Here's what to do:**

### Gather a Core Team

**The Chosen Study Team is a small group with a big purpose.** Draw together a core group made up of those who have seen something "different" in Jesus and want others to experience that difference. The team meets together regularly (shoot for weekly) to support the group process and pray. They plan, oversee the food, and invite friends and family to join in. This team can take on the following roles:

– **The Group Leader** oversees the group's study and discussion process and seeks to foster one-on-one friendship evangelism and discipleship within the group. We encourage the Group Leader to model servant/leadership within the group and to send out weekly emails.

– **The Prayer Team Promoter** finds ways to support the Study in prayer.

– **The Meal Organizer** oversees the food. See *Resources* at the website for theme potluck sign-up sheets. Meal Organizers can also keep in touch during the week with group emails. (The first meal will likely be something like a pizza instead of a planned potluck.)

–**Child Care Helper** for younger families who need such help to come.

–**Set-Up/Sign-Up/Name Tag/Greeter** should be designated, especially for larger groups. For the people who may not feel comfortable at first, you'll want to extend hospitality and friendship from the start.

–**"Tech Person"** to oversee film management—stopping and starting.

–**Small Group Facilitators** (for larger studies—eight or more) oversee their group. **It is best to sit around small tables with just four to six others** (and best to separate spouses), rotating members weekly.

–**Day-Long or Weekend Event Organizer** (see the website).

**FYI:** There are two series: **The Chosen Series** that follows *The Chosen,* and **The Bible Series** which includes other film and passage selections from the Gospels and various books of Scripture. (See pages 180-183 and the website for these options.)

## Be Inclusive of Everyone

**Who to invite?** Everyone who is open to come: The religious, the skeptics, the non-religious, the seekers—you name it. This is to be a fun, interactive place that values and respects everyone.

We hope group members share differences of opinion and viewpoints from all over the spiritual map. We're glad for that to happen. Each person brings their own background. We're not here to judge. We love to stir up discussion and hear unaccustomed perspectives. As Jesus said to Simon in episode seven: *Get used to different!*

**Sharing and Prayer:** To respect where people are spiritually, encourage believers to **avoid insider-type sharing**—which can characterize typical Bible study groups. (Also, prayer should primarily take place before you come or after you leave, not during group time.) A Chosen Study is a **skeptic- and seeker-friendly outreach group** for mutual learning, and to develop deeper friendships both inside and outside the group context.

## Get the Word Out

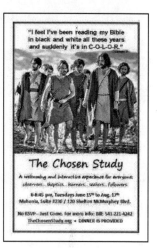

**Direct Invitation:** Yes, we still do that, right?! Indeed, it is by far the most effective means.

**Email Invitation:** Get the word out quickly by sending a link to the trailer, website, and a flyer attachment.

**Text Invitation:** Send out a photo, or better yet, a digital photo (JPG) of your flyer, and an active link to the trailer and website.

**Flyers:** Contact us at our website to receive sample flyers in MS Word that you can adapt and print or make up your own to hand out.

**Create a Facebook Event** and **Church Announcements** for the masses.

## Plan for Food

Our studies seek to connect us to God AND to each other. What better way to bring people together than by sharing food and conversation? We encourage starting with a meal, potluck or finger food. The role of overseeing the meals is a tremendous service. (See *Potluck Sign-Up Sheets* on the website under *Resources*.)

## Lead/Facilitate the Group

You can begin small—with just one friend, one-on-one, or gather a group. Pray, invite, read, and underline key points on pages 8-12 and 169-176. The leader's notes integrated along the way are for both current and future leaders to gain confidence in how to facilitate their groups.

*Multiply Your Efforts*—through small/large (8+) group combos

**Combining small groups within a larger group:** When a group starts large or grows larger—*to eight or more*—the larger size presents unique opportunities. Small groups provide a *depth* of intimacy which allows members to participate more. Larger group interaction can then draw out the very best insights from the small group discussions to offer a *breadth* of give-and-take sharing.

***Day-Long or Weekend Event Organizer*** (see the website).

This combination **provides for two (shorter) discussion times**, with the best of both dynamics, and gives group leaders the role of a "dialogical" (two-way), not "monological" (one-way), teacher. After each small group time, the leader brings together the larger group for a "check-in" to highlight what was discussed within the small groups.

A small/large group combination **offers a chance for the core team to facilitate the smaller groups**. The goal is to foster a guided conversation. This, likewise, is true for a large group leader on a larger scale. Quality, dialogical teaching brings a soft touch to the group sharing by focusing on the best insights gleaned from the small groups.

Larger groups thus **provide discipleship opportunities** for group members to step into the role of small group facilitators, as part of the core Chosen Study team. The goal is to help equip an increasing number of these leaders to multiply their outreach efforts in the lives of others. The challenge during the group time is to keep up the pace.

If you're currently a group member with such aspirations, feel free to study through the guide notes, go through the website and look for an opportunity to join a team, or to start your own Chosen Study!

*For Leader Support:* jesusstudy.org/contact

The website's primary purpose is to equip current and future leaders to make disciples and provide a community of discipleship for those using *The Chosen* for outreach and growth. *How can we serve you?*

## Eight Group Ground Rules to Enhance Your Experience

1. **The Leader** is a **facilitator** of discussion, guiding the group through questions rather than statements. He or she is responsible to **prepare for and oversee group interaction** and to **help with outreach**.

2. **The Guide** makes for a valuable personal study but is especially set up to help **current and future leaders** facilitate watching, study, and discussion in one-to-one, and in small/large group settings.

3. **Prior Preparation** is not expected. We do, however, have a **Drive it Home** reflection time and **Video Insights** for post-Study follow-up.

4. **Each Group Member** "owns the group," and is thus seen as a key contributor of comments and questions. **Talkative members** should defer to others and **quiet members**, speak out. *The conversation engagement around the circle should look like a pinball machine!*

5. **Group Focus** is controlled by its purpose. *The Chosen* Study allows the episode and Scripture passage to **govern the discussion**, rather than Bible commentaries or cross referencing. Tangents are to be avoided or at least "tabled," until after the group meeting is over.

6. **Personal Growth** from studying Jesus is our goal. Such growth naturally includes a **focus on humility** and **child-like faith**.

7. **Group Growth** happens as **friendships form and deepen**. Members should see themselves as more than just a study group, but as a community where consistency, accountability, self-disclosure, empathy, and reaching out to others are key characteristics.

8. **Avoid making "guest appearances."** Don't let *stay-at-home feelings* or distractions dictate whether you come. **Commit to attend** every meeting. Take this gathering seriously—for you and for others.

*Fight "those feelings" and the distractions by <u>signing this challenge</u>:*

Unless out-of-town or near death's door, I'll be there: _____

*Yes, bear down and GO FOR IT! Your initials here.*

## Eight Don'ts of Leading Group Discussions

You're NOT a teacher, you're *a **facilitator***. To lead a highly productive group discussion, start with what NOT to do and you're halfway there!

1. **Don't answer your own questions.** Otherwise, the group will look to you as "the teacher" rather than "the facilitator." You're not just the questioner. You should participate like any member, but don't be the first one to answer your own question.

2. **Don't over-talk.** Groups with an overtalkative leader will often sit back—in boredom! 90% of what we hear we forget, but 90% of what we say, we remember. So, your goal is to get your group talking. Get them remembering. Get them learning.

3. **Don't be afraid of silence.** Silence may mean you need to rephrase the question, but if you "bail out your group" when silent, you set a bad precedent. To exercise patience, count in your head from 100 to 0 before answering—then, only if you must. Oh, yes, they'll talk!

4. **Don't be content with just one answer.** For every written question feel free to ask a follow-up question or two, like: "Does anyone else have a thought?" This allows several people to respond.

5. **Don't expect group members to respond with an answer each time.** They'll be tempted to look straight at you solely, especially when the group is new. Instead, you want them talking to each other, so you don't have to be the "discussion hub" (see page 176).

6. **Don't reject an answer as wrong.** Respond to questionable answers by asking, "How did you come to that conclusion?" or "There's probably a difference of opinion here. Does anyone else have another way of looking at this?" Be affirming to everyone.

7. **Don't be afraid of controversy.** Different opinions are a good thing.

8. **Don't allow the group to end late.** If the discussion proves fruitful, end on time. Don't let the group drag on, but for those who choose to stay, give opportunity to discuss the issue in more depth.

## Eight Do's of Leading Group Discussions

You don't need to be an expert or trained teacher to lead a discussion group. Your role is that of a **facilitator**, one who guides others into a productive conversation centering on key points of the film clips and Bible studies. It's an honor to be able to serve your group in this way.

1. **Bring along your own curiosity and have fun with it.** Good start!

2. **Pace the study.** It's the leader's responsibility to both start and end on time. Keep up a flexible pace with one eye on the clock and the other on the content. There may be more questions than you have time for; so, if necessary, skip some questions. Press ahead!

3. **Give members the chance to study on their own.** They are free to do so—or not. There is no expectation of prior preparation.

4. **Have the Scripture read aloud.** Ask a group member to read. Some feel uncomfortable doing so in public, so don't make a surprise assignment unless you know they are willing and are good at it.

5. **Be on the alert for overtalkative people.** Someone who over-talks can squeeze the life out of a group. If this is a problem, engage with that group member after the meeting, and enlist their help to join you in your goal to get everyone involved in the discussion.

6. **Involve everyone, more or less equally.** Sit across from quiet people to draw them out, and next to talkative people to make less eye contact. If helpful, go around the circle with a question.

7. **Keep the discussion on track by avoiding tangents**. Tangents may seem important but can hurt purposeful discussion, leading the group to talk about less important things. "Important tangents" provide opportunities for conversation outside the group's time.

8. **Conduct a discussion first with general, then specific questions.** Your goal in NOT to get into one-and-done responses; rather, your goal is to start an engaging dialogue with several people responding to a particular question in a back-and-forth way (see next page).

## Facilitating Group Interaction: Monological vs. Dialogical

If tables (small round or rectangle) are available, they are preferred for the meals and for group study (of ideally four to six participants each).

**Dialogical interaction** engages wide-ranging participation. Such give-and-take discussion sparked by the *table leader* and the *upfront leader* is desired. **Interaction from a leader's question is visualized below:**

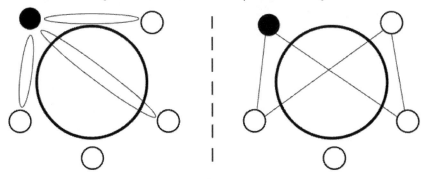

Inferior Monological Interaction    Superior Dialogical Interaction

*Small/Larger Group Combination — Can Work with Eight or More*

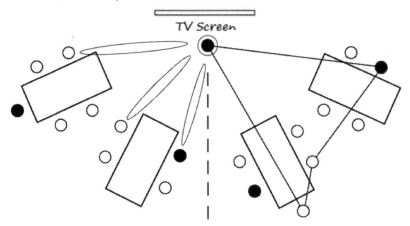

TV Screen

**Dialogical leading** *facilitates interaction* among your group members and prevents you from "brokering" the participants' comments with your own or monopolizing the discussion as seen above. As a leader you can participate, but your goal is to get others talking. **Remember:** 90% of what you say they'll forget, but 90% of what you get them to say, they'll remember! So, get them get them talking and learning!!

Have you seen something different in Jesus? Join a Jesus Study Team and consider becoming a **Jesus Study Leader**

## Leader's Notes: What applies most to you and your group?

-
-
-
-
-
-

## Your Chosen Group: Names, info., prayer concerns, etc.

-
-
-
-
-
-
-

**Your Chosen Group:** Names, info., prayer concerns, etc.

-
-
-
-
-
-
-
-
-
-
-
-
-
-
-
-

**Note:** For a sign-up sheet to print off, see the website under *Resources*.

# Study Resources

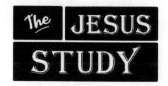

We have a variety of guides available on Amazon or other retailers. Check the website for volume discounts: jesusstudy.org/order-guides

## The Chosen Study Library

*For: skeptics... observers... seekers... learners... followers.*

## THE CHOSEN STUDY
### 10 Studies from 8 Episodes in Each Guide

Season 1   Season 2   Season 3   Season 4   Season 5   Season 6   Season 7

WATER     HOPE      FOOD      SIGHT

## THE BIBLE IN THE CHOSEN
### 20 Studies from 20 Scenes in Each Guide

Season 1   Season 2   Season 3   Season 4   Season 5   Season 6   Season 7

**Find the (eventual) 140 YouTube Chosen Scene Playlist at:**
tinyurl.com/chosen-playlist-1 **(others: -2, -3, -4, -5, -6, -7)**

# THE CHOSEN SERIES (8 Episodes in 10 Studies each)

**SEVEN Chosen Studies** (watching full episodes blended with texts)

*The Chosen Study:* **Season One,** focuses on Simon, Matthew, Andrew, Nicodemus, and Mary Magdalene as they encounter Jesus. This guide, based on the *The Chosen*, covers all the backstory and will give you and your group an in-depth appreciation of his followers' unexpected changes of fortune in getting to know him.

*The Chosen Study:* **Season Two,** guides you and your group into Act Two of Jesus' life and ministry with his followers unsure of where this is all going.

Here we meet the remaining disciples, such as Nathanael, who is despondent over a career in shambles, only to be given a new vocation by Jesus. Besides him, there are a host of others with physical, mental, and emotional infirmities and demon-possession that, up to now, have been impossible to overcome.

*The Chosen Study:* **Season Three,** picks up with the famous *Sermon on the Mount* which sets the stage for the disciples taking a deep look into their own spiritual lives. The Study concludes with the *Feeding of the 5000* and with Jesus and Simon walking on the water.

*The Chosen Study:* **Season Four** continues with Jesus and the disciples finding increasing opposition to Jesus' messianic claims especially from the Jewish religious leaders.

*The Chosen Study:* **Seasons Five, Six and Seven** completes the most audacious story ever told. We look forward to watching the *The Chosen's* version.

## THE BIBLE SERIES (20 Scenes in 20 Studies each)

**SEVEN The Bible in The Chosen** (less backstory, scenes with passages)

**–SEASON ONE Study Guide**          **–SEASON TWO Study Guide**

**These guides** take individuals or groups through Bible passages directly referenced throughout *The Chosen*. In so doing, much of the backstory is left out and a scene playlist is used instead. See the Youtube playlists at: tinyurl.com/chosen-playlist

**–SEASONS THREE, FOUR, FIVE, SIX and SEVEN**

## One-Time Chosen Christmas Event

**Christmas with The Chosen: Holy Night** This episode can be used as a *come-one-come-all event* (content starts at 31:00) before Christmas. Watching and discussing this episode could also act as a winter-quarter (January) kickoff for a new group: tinyurl.com/chosen-christmas

## Going Inward: The Chosen Devotionals

**The Chosen: 40 Days with Jesus** provides a new devotional for each season to extend your experience throughout the week. You divide the 40 devotional readings into five per week: thechosengifts.com

# THE BIBLE SERIES for other "Jesus Films"

We're spoiled by *The Chosen*, but there are other quality, biblical movies, and *Jesus films* out there which we have adapted in a similar way to *The Chosen Study*:

**The John Study** is a ten-week series based on the 2003 movie entitled *The Life of Jesus*. This three-hour film is a word-for-word portrayal of John's Gospel from the *Good News Bible* translation: tinyurl.com/the-john-study-guide

**The Risen Study** is likewise a ten-week series based on a 2016 film entitled *RISEN*. This study follows the movie which begins with Jesus' death on the cross. A religious leader is granted permission to have him buried in his family's tomb and Pontius Pilate posts guards to ensure rumors of "a resurrection" don't take hold in Jerusalem.

When the tomb ends up empty, Pilate's tribune, Clavius, is tasked with finding the body. In the process Clavius finds much more.

**The Paul Study** is a ten-week series based on a 2018 film entitled *Paul: Apostle of Christ*. Our study follows the movie with Paul in a Roman prison near the end of his life. Other local believers struggle with intensely hostile authorities toward them as well.

Luke, Paul's former traveling companion, is desperate to find Paul and to help him get a written record of the gospel out to the world he will soon leave behind.

**The John, Risen and Paul studies make for a superb three-part series.**

## Bible apps, online access

   Excellent for reading: YouVersion.com
Excellent for studying: BilbeGateway.com
Excellent for learning: BibleProject.com

## Going Deeper: Journaling NT

Apply the *Mark-It-Up* study method to the entire New Testament with this double-spaced format for study and note-taking. To find out more about this NT: tinyurl.com/journal-nt

# THE COUPLE SERIES

**Are you getting all the romance, passion and joy you want in your relationship?** Wouldn't you like to.....

- *Tell your partner how he or she can fully love you?*
- *Be fully listened to and completely understood in the process?*
- *Be nurtured and cherished in the unique way you feel loved?*

**When it comes to the opposite sex, the intimacy rules are different!**

This book will help you understand and overcome those differences by sharing an ordinary couple's extraordinary weekend of intimate conversations.

Sarah and Matt get away from the house, the kids and their daily lives to listen to each other's hearts, explore their differences and deepen their connection. Intimate Conversations enhances the lessons of their free-wheeling dialogue with practical how-to sections inviting readers to explore their own hearts and those of their partners: tinyurl.com/for-couples

# Leadership Resources

Our desire is to help church pastoral staff equip leaders to facilitate vibrant, "evangelizing, discipleship" communities that draw people in to watch, discover and relate to Jesus. When it comes to these studies, we've been there, done that. So, let us know how we can serve you.

## Why make the change from Bible Study 1.0 to Bible Study 2.0?

"Bible Study 1.0"—with its cognitive, all-talk, text-heavy or once-over-lightly approach—is what many of us grew up with and loved.

But this approach is not reaching our visual generation who instead seek visible learning via YouTube, video games, zoom, and webinar broadcasts on our devices. This visual experience has completely taken over our lives, shrunk our attention spans, and yes, become the basis of most learning for every generation.

Into this milieu, enter "Bible Study 2.0," aka, *The Jesus Study*. Which begs the question: **What makes The Jesus Study different?**

Our initial answer is this:
**Integrating film and video with Scripture**

Films such as *The Chosen, The Life of Jesus* (John's Gospel), *RISEN,* and *Paul: Apostle of Christ*—each with the underlying Scriptures crafted into a ten-week experience.
To that jumping-off point we add three distinctives:

*Jesus-centeredness*

*Personal growth through an evangelizing discipleship focus*

*Inductive, mark-it-up study*

Those foundational traits are expanded in *twelve qualities* common to Jesus Studies. This distinguishing blend makes for a unique Bible study and God-encountering experience.

## Twelve Distinctives of Jesus Studies

1. **Designed to be Jesus-centered** in the personal study, discussion and the "at home," quiet time experience.

2. **Intentionally includes an evangelizing discipleship focus** as a dual priority for personal and ministry growth among members.

3. **Combines film with complementary Scripture** passages along with **worship and teaching videos** to include visual elements of learning.

4. **Offers a skeptic- and seeker-friendly environment** to talk about Jesus among friends and colleagues in a ten-week time frame.

5. **Encourages food inclusion at each gathering** to facilitate connection among group members in a relaxed environment.

6. **Forms a core group that prays and prepares** to lead the various aspects of the group process and to spearhead outreach efforts.

7. **Embeds all Old and New Testament texts** into the guides for ready reference, especially for those unfamiliar with the Bible.

8. **Uses a four-colored BIC pen to mark up the texts** which employs an inductive mindset for observing, interpreting and applying Scripture.

9. **Ends with a fun and memorable (paper) T-Shirt Design** each week that summarizes and crystallizes the learning process.

10. **Incorporates Drive it Home and Video Insights sections** after the study for additional, "at home," video learning opportunities.

11. **Grows Jesus-followers into group leaders** with dialogical facilitating skills and both a discipleship and evangelistic framework for ministry.

12. **Encourages leaders to equip others to lead new studies** within their own circles of influence of friends, family, and coworkers.

## Take our No-Cost Bible Study 2.0 Orientation Session or Leadership Course

**The Jesus Study is a 2.0 "evangelizing discipleship" experience.** Again, what does this mean? *In a nutshell we combine film with Mark-It-Up Scripture study and invite our non-church friends to join us.* To help you excel at doing this we'd like to have you join us on Zoom... OR...

We could also arrange to travel and meet up with you and your leadership team. We are serious about training and will work out what we can to assure you are equipped. Such help will give you a strong running start to your efforts.

### How to Lead and Promote Your Group

Though years in the making, *The Jesus Study* formally came together on May 28, 2021, in a Zoom call led by Bill Syrios with some gifted Bible study leaders. Get in on that call and learn to lead in the process: tinyurl.com/lead-your-group

Here's a four-minute introduction to *The Chosen Study*. Pages 8-12 (especially page 9) in the guide lay out the methodology for your first gathering. The template for leading the studies is on pages 17-18: tinyurl.com/intro-your-group

## Our Mission: What We're About

The Jesus Study combines film depiction with Scripture in a welcoming and interactive experience for all: observers... skeptics... learners... seekers... followers, who WATCH > DISCOVER > RELATE together the Most Audacious Story ever told.

## Our Executive Leadership Team: What We Do

*We work with leaders, to help them create a friendly place to watch > discover > relate.*

*Back to Front, Left to Right:*

Dave Hawkins, Tori Foss and Dietrich Gruen
Bill & Teresa Syrios and
Cathy & Don Baker

## Our Invitation: Zoom with us - Start a Group - Join the Team

Do you have some loaves and fish to bring to this endeavor? We are looking for those who have seen "the Jesus' difference" and are interested in exploring how to spread that difference around the world using *The Jesus Study*. If that sounds like you, please contact us.

**Your Faith Journey:**

**Your Faith Journey:**

**Your Faith Journey:**

Made in the USA
Columbia, SC
08 January 2025

51434924R00107